Library of Congress Cataloging-in-Publication Data

Lion House weddings.
    p.   cm.
    Includes index.
    ISBN 1-57345-972-0 (alk. paper)
    1. Weddings—Planning.   2. Weddings—Equipment and supplies.   3. Wedding etiquette.   4. Quantity cookery.   I. Lion House (Restaurant)

HQ745.L55 2003
395.2'2—dc21   2002154085

Printed in the United States of America   42316-6825
Inland Press, Menomonee Falls, WI

10   9   8   7   6   5   4   3   2   1

Lion House Weddings

Text by
Jennifer Adams

Photography by
Alan Blakely
John Luke

EAGLE GATE
SALT LAKE CITY, UTAH

Contents

Acknowledgments

The work of many people goes into the making of a book.

A debt of gratitude goes to Geri Tiedemann, general manager of the Lion House; Dianne Theurer, general manager of the Joseph Smith Memorial Building; and Spencer Herzog, vice president of food service operations for the Temple Square Hospitality Corporation. Thanks also to the chefs of the Lion House and Joseph Smith Memorial Building, most especially Julie Ulrich, Brenda Hopkin, David Bench, Don Sanchez, and Steve Kachocki, who spent many hours pulling together recipes for the book.

I appreciate the many photographers whose work is included in this book, including John Luke and Alan Blakely. Also thanks to Design Werks of Bountiful, who provided many photographs as well as props and decorations for photo shoots, and to Maxine Bramwell, the food stylist.

Several outstanding bakeries made beautiful wedding cakes to be photographed for *Lion House Weddings:* Ambrosia, Bakers de Normandie, Carrie's Cakes, Exclusive Cakes by Barbara, Mrs. Backer's Pastry Shop, Mrs. Flinder's Cakes, Pastry Arts Barrani, and the wonderful bakers at the Lion House and Joseph Smith Memorial Building.

Flowers are at the heart of a wedding, and I owe special thanks to the following florists who contributed time and lovely arrangements for the book: Beverly Olson at Brown Floral, Tami Long at Huddart Floral, and Colleen Hanson, Lori Gillespie Hansen, and Cynthia Bodily at the Joseph Smith Memorial Building. And especially to Rachael MacLaughlin-Howells at Roots, my own florist who helped make my wedding beautiful and who I appreciate and admire.

At Deseret Book, I express thanks to Jana Erickson for her dedication and patience. I will always be grateful to her for giving me the opportunity to write this book at the point in time she did. Thanks to Shauna Gibby for her work in art direction and design and to Tonya Facemyer for typesetting. I am especially grateful to Janna DeVore. She spent countless hours reworking text and reconciling many differing opinions. She is a fine editor and a true friend.

Your wedding reception will be one of the most remembered events of your life—a commemoration of love and happiness to share with those most dear to you. It's a time of celebration and a crescendo of months of careful planning and anxious anticipation. Whether you are planning an elaborate event with many guests or an intimate dinner for only family and close friends, this book will help you plan the perfect wedding reception—from the big decisions down to the smallest details. Pore over the ideas provided and adapt them to your personal tastes and styles. Remember, this is your moment, your chance to create the day of your dreams.

TYPES OF RECEPTIONS

After you set a wedding date, one of the most crucial decisions you must make is what type of reception you will have. Do you want a traditional wedding reception with many guests and a formal receiving line? Or would you prefer a more informal open house? You may decide that a small gathering for a formal dinner, in lieu of a traditional reception, is better suited to your tastes and style. Many brides have a reception in the bride's hometown and an open house given by the parents of the groom two or three weeks later.

The location for your celebration will greatly influence the type of reception you choose to have. Some brides have their receptions in historic homes or churches; others opt for a quaint garden setting or a romantic gathering on a beach. The Lion House and the Joseph Smith Memorial Building, each with its own history and style, are lovely settings for an unforgettable reception. Meetinghouses, family backyards, and reception centers can also be transformed into elegant settings that reflect your individuality. Each of these sites lends itself to a different kind of wedding reception. As you determine the type of reception you'd like, consider how many people you want to invite, the number of people you want to include in the wedding party, the

Color plays a significant role in the formality of any wedding reception.
TOP: Crisp white linens, classic roses, and small pewter vases add to the
elegance of this very formal reception at the Joseph Smith Memorial Building.
BOTTOM: Cheerful yellows and blue gingham checks inspire a casual and
relaxed gathering.

kind and amount of food you want to serve, what type of music you prefer, if there will be dancing, and so on.

CHOOSING A STYLE OR THEME

Selecting a style or theme for your reception may seem as elusive as finding the perfect pair of shoes for your wedding gown. It is, however, an important part of creating a beautiful, cohesive reception. A number of things can serve as the starting point for determining your wedding theme, from the style of your gown to your favorite variety of flowers to the season in which you will marry. But it is of overriding importance once you have established a theme or style to keep the rest of your reception in harmony with this decision. The style or theme you select will help dictate other choices, such as which type of flowers you carry, how formal your announcements should be, what your bridesmaids will wear, and so on.

The style of your wedding should reflect your personality and preferences. And remember, even though some of these decisions will seem overwhelming or insignificant—and everyone from your own mother to your soon-to-be sister-in-law will have their own ideas—these are happy decisions. This is your opportunity to personalize your wedding and thus make it the event you always dreamed it would be.

Formality

The degree of formality you wish to create plays a large role in your wedding's style. For example, if you know you want an elegant dress, several bridesmaids in

Paper lanterns are a pretty and economical decoration for outdoor receptions. The garden setting at this reception needs minimal decorations and no table settings, as guests can simply seat themselves and wait to be served small refreshment plates.

formal attire, and a string quartet playing in the background then you have already pinned down the type of wedding you want. You need only determine the details that will finalize your theme. Your reception may include a traditional wedding cake, bridesmaids carrying nosegays, and elaborate refreshments. On the other hand, if you prefer a garden wedding with no receiving line, or if you want to wear a simple dress and have a small reception, you will likely select a different style. Decorations at a casual reception might include balloons, and your invitations may be casual and colorful—using modern fonts and folding techniques—rather than traditional. Food at a less-formal gathering could be a light buffet or an ice cream sundae.

Color

You should select a color scheme for your wedding early on, and this will guide you in making other choices. Your colors can be carried through to every detail of the wedding. The wedding cake, flowers, wedding party attire, tablecloths, chair covers, centerpieces, and even wedding favors all offer opportunities to carry your color scheme throughout your reception.

Of course, it's wise to use taste and to carefully balance colors when you are designing your reception. Consider using your wedding color intermittently with complementary colors. If you have chosen pink, for example, you may not want your entire wedding to be pink and thus overwhelming in color. Perhaps bridesmaids could wear the color, but mothers of the bride and groom could dress in cream or pearly gray. Or bridesmaids could wear a complementary color and carry pink flowers as an accent. Tablecloths could be pink—or they could be white, with a pink napkin or pink and white flowers for centerpieces. Your cake

LEFT: Deep purple bows and vibrant red, yellow, and purple flowers add just the right touch of color to this reception. RIGHT: A variety of flowers—yellow enchantment lilies, lisianthus, and freesia, red roses, and purple hyacinth and stock—spill over a simple silver compote.

Color can be used to unify the elements of any wedding gathering. Here, a subtle pink ribbon accents white tablecloths, while goblets of pink punch and soft pink roses in the bouquet and on the cake complement each other.

Autumn brides can take advantage of the rich fall foliage and colors by incorporating them into unique centerpieces like this one, which includes wheat, dried protea, gomphrena, pods, and rust-colored straw flowers.

could have a pale pink frosting, accented with white orchids, rather than a white cake topped with the obvious pink carnations and roses.

Some color schemes carry additional meaning. A black and white color scheme, for example, usually indicates a more formal wedding reception than a variety of pastels used together.

Brides often choose a color based on the particular flowers they want to carry or the season in which they are marrying, while others have a favorite color that they know they will use for their reception from the time they get engaged.

Season

The season in which you marry plays a significant role in the style or theme of your wedding. It can influence everything from the type of wedding gown you choose to the food you will serve. Flowers, menus, fabrics, decorations—all these are influenced by the colors, hues, and textures of the season. When setting your wedding date, don't forget to take this into account.

Short-sleeved bridal gowns made of lighter fabrics, such as silk or organza, are popular in the spring and summer. And lighter colors are often chosen for the wedding party during these seasons. For fall and winter weddings, fabrics for gowns might include brocades, satins, and taffetas. Warm earth tones might be worn by the bridal party in fall and rich reds or deep greens in winter. Be sure to read the chapter on Food for ideas on the different types of food that work best for different seasons. Also review the chapter on Flowers for ideas on which flowers work well in which seasons.

TOP: A glass bowl spilling over with gold ornaments is accented by a sprig of Christmas greenery. BOTTOM: This classic black chair takes on a holiday look when tied with a sheer, shimmering ribbon and decked out with red ornaments and pine boughs.

TOP LEFT: *Pink tulips and tall green grass combine in this fun spring arrangement. Brides might choose to replicate the arrangement by placing small pots of grass and a single tulip at each guest's plate.* TOP RIGHT: *Summer's abundance is shown off in this vivid display of fruits and flowers. A presentation of luscious strawberries, grapes, apples, and pineapples would look particularly stunning in the center of a buffet table at a formal wedding dinner or afternoon lunch.* BOTTOM LEFT: *A wrought-iron chair and a few simple fall decorations reflect the deep orange and brown colors of autumn. Setting up a few props in front of a door creates a nice location for placing gifts at a home reception or open house and also lets guests know that a particular door is not to be used as a thoroughfare.* BOTTOM RIGHT: *Christmas colors are not the only options for a winter wedding. Lavenders and mauves provide beautiful accents to a silver and white wedding. Other decorations could include crystal snowflakes, frosted glass balls, and shimmery white ribbons tied around candles or lampposts.*

Seasonal holidays also influence wedding themes. If you are getting married at Christmastime, you will want to consider Christmas trees as a decorative backdrop to your wedding. Red or forest-green satin, tartan plaids, and dark velvets are fabrics that lend themselves to wedding party attire for this season. Yellow tulips would look out of place at Christmastime, as would summery bridesmaid gowns. But if your heart is set on a certain flower or color that is not in season, consider creative ways to make the color work with the time of year. For example, if you want your color to be lavender in December, use Christmas trees decorated with purple ornaments, or have bridesmaids wearing lavender gowns but carrying dark, lush greenery. Use silver as a color to complement the lavender.

Other

You may have personal tastes and interests that lend themselves to a "theme wedding." For example, some couples choose a country or western-style wedding, featuring small cowboy hats as table centerpieces, with the groom wearing black cowboy boots and a bolo tie. Other brides may have a love for a specific country or culture and use that to dictate their wedding's style. Consider a Scottish theme, where the bridesmaids are dressed in the family tartan and a bagpiper provides the music; or a Hawaiian theme, where luau food is served and the bridesmaids wear leis instead of carrying bouquets.

A single, simple detail can also be used to carry your theme throughout the reception. For example, a tiny heart could grace the wedding announcement and the refreshment napkin. Heart-shaped confetti could then be

TOP LEFT: Reception decorations can be as simple as a dozen carefully placed trees lit up with tiny white lights and an artful arrangement of greenery and branches to flank the entryway. TOP RIGHT: Many brides stray from the traditional by creating a theme for their special day. If, for example, you are married near the 4th of July, you may choose to use a vivid display of red, whites, and blues in your flowers, decorations, and refreshments.

sprinkled on the tables for a colorful centerpiece and tossed at the couple as they leave the reception. Or a flower, such as a daisy, can be twined into wreaths for the flower girls' heads, used in the bridal bouquet, and re-created as tiny fondant flowers on the wedding cake.

DECORATING

Wedding decorations add romance, ambiance, and style to your setting, from bows tied on lampposts to white lights that twinkle in the night air. Select decorations to match your wedding colors and then dress up your setting as little or as much as you like.

Lighting

People often overlook the importance of lighting as a decorative element in a wedding. It is so subtle, yet so significant. Lighting alone can change the whole mood of a wedding. Proper lighting will enable your guests to see all the details of the setting. Lighting that is too bright or harsh can create a setting that lacks intimacy or makes guests feel exposed, while lighting that is too dark or shadowy can feel somber. Too much artificial light in wide open settings can feel depressing.

There are many ways to add the right amount of light to your setting. Hurricane lamps, torches, candelabras, candles on brass or silver candlesticks, votive holders, and luminaries are all options.

White lights strung on tree branches, plants, railings, arbors, or even under sheer table toppers add a magical effect. Consider lighting the path to a garden reception with luminaries—small paper bags filled with sand to weigh them down and a small votive candle placed within each bag. The paper bags can even have stenciled or cutout patterns on them, or can be inscribed

LEFT: This exotic theme is perfect for a formal wedding dinner. The simple white tablecloth is draped with stunning fabrics. Small votive candles are wrapped with greenery and tied with a simple piece of raffia for favors at each plate. Formal, yet unusual flowers such as birds of paradise, anthurium, pincushion proteus, and braided emerald leaves, make a beautiful centerpiece. RIGHT: Most craft stores have materials that can be used to create a variety of greenery. These trees are wrapped in sheer white tulle and held in simple wooden boxes. Two or three in a row on each side of the door make a nice impression and let guests know they've come to the right entry.

Lighting is the best way to add a little magic to any setting. Candles, hurricane lamps, luminaries, and paper lanterns each add warmth to a room. It's really all in the details: line a walkway to the reception hall with hanging lanterns, keep votive candles burning at each of the guest tables as well as at any serving or display tables, decorate trees and railings with tiny white lights.

A striking array of summer flowers—classic pink roses, towering lavender stock and white delphinium, purple liatrus, and large white lilies—sit atop stately white columns at the base of an archway entwined with full pink and white roses and sheer tulle. This corner display provides a fragrant setting for the bride and groom to greet and thank their guests at a garden reception.

with the couple's initials. Luminaries are equally charming in summer as in winter.

Candles add formality and light to any table; they are the simplest way to add drama to an event. Candles should be lit before guests arrive and stay lighted until they leave. Be sure wicks are trimmed to keep candles from giving off black smoke. Candles displayed on breakfast or luncheon tables are generally not lit, but are used for decoration, as formal etiquette states that candles should not be lit in the daytime. However, candles do add warmth at any time of the day and individual preference can dictate in this matter.

Another way to effectively use lighting is to spotlight certain elements of the reception. You can spotlight an ice sculpture with colored gels to show its translucency and give it color, or light each table with a spotlight from above to emphasize the table decor.

When considering lighting on food, the color of the light should be taken into consideration. Blue and green lighting makes food look discolored and unappealing. Keep to amber or soft white or pink when lighting food. Remember that soft light adds romance and a sense of comfort to your setting.

Props

Many brides choose a formal backdrop for their receiving line. White lattice trellises, columns, archways, ficus trees with white lights, gazebos, canopies, and other formal backdrops grace your setting and set apart the wedding line with the importance it deserves. In outdoor receptions, consider using small, romantic footbridges. At Christmastime, use rows of fresh cut pine trees.

TOP: Most wedding caterers can set up and decorate glorious outdoor receptions with the use of grand white canopies and linens. A canopy provides a more intimate setting for large wedding dinners and protects food—and guests—from harsh heat or heavy breezes. BOTTOM: Gazebos and pavilions can be decorated with floral garlands and sheer tulle to create beautiful settings for cake tables, buffet tables, or ice sculptures.

Flowers

The floral displays that surround you at your reception weave magic and romance throughout the room and set the mood of the occasion like almost nothing else can. Your wedding's theme will provide the direction for floral decorations. Floral tabletop arrangements should echo the bridal bouquet and should be lower than eye level to accommodate conversation. Towering topiaries of fresh flowers at gift and buffet tables can create an informal feeling. Consider using wreaths and garlands on doorways and railings. Flower petals can be strewn on the display table for the wedding cake or piled around fruit platters on the buffet table. Fresh cut flowers as well as potted flowers are appropriate, and flowers growing in flowerbeds at outdoor weddings should not be overlooked as part of the decorations.

Ice Sculptures

A popular trend in wedding décor is ice sculptures. Individual carvings can be placed on each table, or larger carvings can be used to highlight the food at a buffet or as a centerpiece for the room. Ice sculptures can be very heavy; make sure to reinforce tables before placing ice on display. Sculptures should be set out an hour in advance of the event so that the ice will begin to melt and the shape will become clear. Another way to use ice sculptures is as a display for food. Shrimp or crab legs can be beautifully displayed in a carved ice shell. If you do this, however, remember not to reuse the ice with other food at a later date.

Other

Balloons, mirror balls, streamers, satin or taffeta bows, hay bales, pumpkins and gourds, fresh cut branches of cherry blossoms, vases of pussy willows, love birds in a decorative cage, Christmas trees, candles,

Any number of small details will add elegance to your wedding reception. ABOVE LEFT: Tie a wide white ribbon around each chair back and tuck a single rose in the knot. ABOVE MIDDLE: Attach a nosegay of vibrant flowers to tall candle stanchions placed at the entrance to your reception hall. ABOVE RIGHT: Add an ice sculpture to your cake table or buffet table.

This weathered birdcage, decorated with ivy and a creamy ribbon, adds a charming touch to the gift table or book table at an outdoor wedding. A small bunch of purple hydrangea adds a subtle touch of color to an otherwise monochromatic theme.

and endless other things can be used as decorations for your reception. Be creative and remember to coordinate your decorations with your wedding theme.

MUSIC

Music brings both personal and emotional elements to your wedding reception and can be used to create the perfect mood for your setting. Background music is important not only because it sets the atmosphere but also because it fills in space that might otherwise feel too quiet and empty. It allows guests to feel comfortable and to relax.

Many brides have CD players playing classical or romantic music in the background; others bring in a string quartet or hire a professional piano player for the evening. Some brides even hire a live band to play background music for the reception and then, at the end of the reception, play music for dancing.

Music can include songs with special meaning for the bride and groom and is a great way to add a very personal touch. At one wedding, a bride's best friend was a jazz musician and brought his band to play as his gift to the couple. At another wedding, a daughter of a first marriage played the piano, performing songs she had written for her mother's remarriage.

ORGANIZING YOUR SETTING

The key to a well-executed reception is in the planning. Plan in advance; enlist the right help. Employing adequate staffing to execute your plans is vital to a successful, low-stress event. Your catering staff should work almost invisibly at the reception to make sure the evening runs smoothly.

For plated meals, plan on one server for every twenty to twenty-four guests. If you do not have this server-to-guest ratio, the service will be slow and inefficient and guests may feel neglected or impatient. When scheduling a reception center, plan on at least five servers for the reception. For receptions with over four hundred guests, add one additional server per each one hundred additional guests. You should assign either a server or wedding hostess to handle the specific needs of the bridal party, from bringing water to those in the receiving line to managing the details of cutting the cake.

Another element of a well-organized reception is the comfortable flow of space. Organize tables so people can move comfortably between them. Tables with too much distance from each other feel isolated, while tables placed too close together feel cramped. Place the receiving line in a well-chosen spot that doesn't cause a bottleneck in the entranceway. Guests should be able to enter

OPPOSITE: This beautiful garden reception at the Lion House is decorated with a potpourri of summer flowers. A lush grapevine is wrapped around the wrought-iron rails near the stairs and entwined with tiny white lights. Flowers at each table and in the wreath on the outside wall include yellow, lavender, pink, and red roses, yellow snapdragons, cobalt blue veronica, orange lilies, pink hyacinth, and seeded eucalyptus. Each chair back is tied with a length of sheer organza fabric.

the reception area, sign the guest book, drop off their gift, move through the wedding line, and be seated for refreshments, all without feeling crowded or being forced to zigzag back and forth.

For wedding breakfasts, luncheons, or dinners, guests should be able to find their assigned seats easily, either by place cards or with the direction of a hostess assigned to this task.

Seating Details

At a formal wedding dinner it is important to have assigned seating because guests will spend a large portion of the reception at their tables. A good hostess should make an effort to determine compatible dinner partners. This can be a challenging task, but it is an important one. Think of the common interests or shared experiences of your guests. For example, you might put all your single friends together, friends from college together, or co-workers from the same company together. Seat guests together whenever a possible connection might be made. Use a pencil for preliminary sketching of the seating arrangements until all RSVPs are in and you have a definite guest list. Have everything ready ahead of time but be prepared for the possibility of last minute changes.

Place cards are an essential part of formal seating arrangements, directing guests to their assigned seats. There are many ways to create place cards that match your wedding theme. A place card can be printed or handwritten on cardstock, which is folded into a small tent and placed at the head of the plate. They can also be combined with favors in a number of creative ways. For ideas on place cards, see the chapter on Favors.

At a formal wedding meal, the bride, groom, and their parents often will sit together at a head table. This table can be either at the center or at one end of the room, or may even be placed on a low dais facing the guests. The bride usually sits on the right side of the groom. The bride's parents are placed next to her, with the groom's parents at his side, alternating men and women. This seating arrangement can be tricky, as divorces and remarriages often come into play. Organize the seating in the best possible way to accommodate the different needs of your guests and yourself. If either you or your fiancé have children from a previous marriage, be sure to include them in your wedding breakfasts, luncheons, and dinners, and all your celebrations. After all, they will be some of the people most affected by your marriage.

TABLE SETTINGS

Whether tables are set for a wedding breakfast or for guests to have refreshment plates as they come and go throughout the evening, the table settings you create should be carefully thought-out and should add to the wedding experience for your guests.

Place Settings

For formal tables remember that the place settings should be placed an equal distance apart, and that each guest should be given adequate space. Eighteen inches, or the width of a banquet chair, is the minimum amount of space between guests to allow adequate room. For round tables, the most comfortable configuration is eight, though some tables can seat ten. An option for

TOP LEFT: *Place cards, such as these simple cards on white cardstock with a pretty printed wedding script, help guests find their seats at formal gatherings and add a personal touch to the table.* TOP RIGHT: *Underneath the napkin at this place setting is a printed program of the evening's celebration.* BOTTOM LEFT: *This very formal place setting includes a number of small details reproduced from the larger floral arrangements throughout the room and from the wedding cake. Tiny, two-layer cakes decorated with smooth fondant frosting and a tiny pewter vase filled with white hydrangea are placed beside each plate.* BOTTOM RIGHT: *This place setting has a more casual feel, achieved by tying the napkin with a sage green wired ribbon and placing small bags of pink mints at each plate.*

smaller wedding parties is putting all the guests together at one long, rectangular table.

The tableware, silverware, and glassware you select indicate the formality of your meal. Sterling silver and crystal should be saved for the most formal weddings. Brightly colored plates, mixed and matched china, and more whimsical centerpieces can help create a more casual table setting.

In place settings the largest glass, or the water glass, stands to the right of the plate, above the knife. The juice glass is placed closer to the plate, between the top of the knife and the water glass. The bread plate sits to the top left of the setting, and the dessert plate is set directly above the dinner plate, or is brought out when the dessert is served.

For flatware and silverware the best rule of thumb to remember when eating is always to work from the outside in. The knife is placed to the right of the plate, the serrated edge facing the plate. The dinner spoon is placed to the right of the knife, the soup spoon to the right of the dinner spoon. The dinner fork is placed to the left of the plate, the salad fork to the left of the dinner fork. Dessert utensils are placed horizontally above the plate. Dessert forks should have the tines facing right; dessert spoons are placed above the fork with the main part of the spoon facing left. Silverware should be spread only far enough to fit a twelve-inch plate between it. Napkins that are not folded above the plate, on the plate, or in the empty water glass should be placed to the left of the plate, under the forks.

Linens

Although often overlooked, linens can be an invaluable component of a beautifully set table. Linens must be clean and pressed. A wrinkled or spotted tablecloth will detract from the elegance of your table setting.

The whole look of a table can depend solely on the way each napkin is folded. LEFT: This simple fold takes on an elegant look when slipped through a brass napkin ring. RIGHT: A bright white fan napkin helps define each place setting at this casual table, which seems perfect for a summer wedding breakfast or early brunch.

White and ivory colored linens are the most formal. Bright colors or patterns are more casual. In fact, a room can be made formal or informal simply by the color and style of linens you choose. A tablecloth should hang down from the table approximately eighteen inches. It is not necessary for it to hang to the floor, however some brides may choose a longer tablecloth to cover the table legs and soften the room's appearance. Colored toppers can be added to white or off-white tablecloths as accents and to tie in with the color scheme of the wedding. Lace overlays add elegance to a table setting.

For formal settings, use linen napkins. They should be twenty-four inches square and match, coordinate, or contrast nicely with the color of the tablecloth. There are many different ways to fold linen napkins—some add height and drama to a place setting; others add whimsy and playfulness. Napkin rings are a fun part of table settings and can be used to dress up a table, to provide a favor, or to carry out a wedding theme. Braided raffia or wire-edged ribbon make nice alternatives to traditional napkin rings.

Tablecloth size chart

TABLE SIZE	CLOTH SIZE	SEATS
SQUARE		
28" to 40"	52" x 52"	4 people
ROUND		
30" to 42"	52" round	4 people
42" to 44"	60" to 68"	4 to 6 people
42" to 54"	68" w/fringe	6 people
42" to 60"	72" round	6 people
64" to 76"	90" round	6 to 8 people
OBLONG		
36" x 54"	52" x 70"	4 to 6 people
42" x 62"	60" x 80"	6 to 8 people
48" x 72"	72" x 90"	6 to 8 people
48" x 90"	72" x 108"	8 to 10 people
OVAL		
36" x 54"	52" x 70"	4 to 6 people
42" x 62"	60" x 80"	6 to 8 people
48" x 72"	72" x 90"	6 to 8 people
48" x 90"	72" x 108"	8 to 10 people

Brides who wish to add an exotic element to a themed wedding dinner might choose from one of these unique place settings. LEFT: A napkin folded like a bird of paradise adds to the striking theme of this black and gold place setting. It also softens the look of the unique leopard print fabric draped across the table. RIGHT: This Asian place setting includes black napkins folded calla-lily style and placed in the glasses at each plate. An authentic silk table topper adds to the drama of the table.

TOP LEFT: *A fragrant gardenia and a round stone are set in this easy-to-make centerpiece.* TOP MIDDLE: *This floral centerpiece repeats the theme used in the bride's bouquet: an array of lavender and white flowers, including roses, tulips, mascari, montecasino, freesia, and statice.* TOP RIGHT: *Two small votive candleholders and three taller glass vases are grouped together to form a contemporary centerpiece.* BOTTOM: *The bride at this reception chose to repeat a beautiful display of roses and lisianthus—in red and deep purple tones—and bright yellow enchantment lilies at each table.*

Centerpieces

Centerpieces are a wonderful way to express your creativity and to carry out your wedding theme. Centerpieces should be low enough that guests can easily see and converse over them. They should enhance the setting, not detract from it. Centerpieces are most often flowers that match the colors and style of the wedding, but other centerpieces, such as fish bowls with live fish, potted herbs, candles, and bowls of candy can also be used. For a dramatic flair, tall centerpieces placed above eye level can be very effective.

GUEST BOOK

Although it is not required by etiquette, most couples choose to have a guest book for their guests to sign, that they can keep as a memento of their wed-

ding. The guest book table is often placed where guests first enter the reception. You can ask a friend, younger sister, or cousin to sit at the table and greet guests; this is a nice way to informally include someone in your wedding party.

Besides an attractive book and pen, tables often hold a flower arrangement (sometimes the bride's toss bouquet is placed here), and a portrait of either the bride or the couple. The book itself can vary from a standard leather-bound guest book to a beautiful handmade paper one. Some couples choose to have a large print of their engagement photograph matted for their guests to sign.

DISPLAYING PHOTOGRAPHS

Many brides wish to display their bridal portrait at the reception. A large portrait is often displayed on an

ABOVE LEFT: A copy of your wedding invitation and the lace handkerchief your mother carried on her wedding day will become treasured mementos of this wonderful day. ABOVE RIGHT: In addition to an attractive pen and a gilded-edge guest book, this table also holds the bride's toss bouquet and a bridal portrait.

easel near the entrance of the reception, or a smaller photograph at the book signing table. Other times the couple's engagement photo is placed at the book signing table. A separate display table can also be used to display pictures of the bride and groom, depicting their childhood and their life together. Some brides will frame pictures of the couple's courtship and place them on each individual table for guests to see. Wedding videos are also popular. The video is usually set up in a convenient, out-of-the-way location to run continuously for guests to view throughout the evening.

GIFT AND FAVOR TABLES

Providing guests a place to leave their gifts is a nice gesture. Place a clothed table in a well-thought-out area for this purpose. Some couples assign two or more young children to greet guests at the door and take their gifts to the table for them. Someone assigned to man the gift table could also affix loose cards to packages with scotch tape. This ensures that cards and gifts are not separated when packages are taken home and will make the task of writing proper thank-you notes much easier.

If you are providing favors for each guest at your reception, you may want to consider placing a table for favors at a convenient spot near the exit of the reception. The grouping of favors can make a lovely table display, whether you have tiny beribboned packages, bunches of fresh herbs, or carefully wrapped candies. See the chapter on Favors for additional ideas.

TOP LEFT: Use your mother's bridal and wedding portraits to inspire you as you plan your own big day. You may even choose to set up a display table at the reception that features your bridal portrait along with nostalgic memorabilia and photographs from your mother's and grandmother's weddings. TOP MIDDLE: Your own bridal portrait can be a stunning decoration at your celebration. Place it in a beautiful frame and display it at the entrance to your reception. TOP RIGHT: Historic buildings make beautiful reception halls. The entrance to this reception is draped with greenery, while the door is left open to make guests feel immediately welcome.

TOP LEFT: *Any number of places can be used to store gifts at a reception: a wooden sleigh, a traditional table, or a park bench, like this one.* TOP RIGHT: *Tiny boxes wrapped in foil and tied with a pretty ribbon make excellent favors and can also double as place cards by attaching a small card to the box.* BOTTOM LEFT: *Pastel dinner mints wrapped in sheer netting and tied with matching bows can be placed at a table near the exit for guests to pick up on their way out.* BOTTOM RIGHT: *If you are giving out favors at the luncheon or wedding dinner, rather than at the reception, consider tying the gifts into your theme. These cute favors hold up the place cards at the luncheon and reflect the bride's choice of bright spring colors.*

*Outdoor receptions lend themselves to a variety of
beautiful backdrops. This wrought-iron, tent-shaped
arbor is flanked by several tall columns and draped with
blooms in bright purple, peach, pink, and white—the
perfect place for a bride and groom to greet their guests.*

RING CEREMONIES

A Latter-day Saint couple may arrange with their bishop to hold a special gathering for relatives and close friends who are not able to attend the temple ceremony. In this intimate setting, the couple might say a few words of commitment and love to each other and then exchange rings, which will help the invited guests feel included in the marriage.

The couple's parents are often invited to give a few words of advice to their newly married children and express their love for them on this important day. Some couples also ask their bishop to conduct and offer advice as well. This is a nice gesture, but is not necessary, since the ring ceremony has no religious implications but is strictly symbolic.

This brief gathering usually takes place before the wedding luncheon or reception begins, and attendance is best limited to those closest to the couple. An elaborate ceremony with the bride walking down the aisle with her father or with bridesmaids is discouraged.

RECEIVING LINE

When organizing your receiving line choose a place that will provide the best flow of space for your reception. Traditionally, the bride's mother stands at the beginning of the line to greet the guests, followed by the bride's father. They are followed by the groom's mother and father. The bride and groom follow them. If there

TOP: *Reception refreshments might include a slice of wedding cake for each guest, or individual cakes that replicate a design used in the actual wedding cake.* BOTTOM: *Brides may choose to set up a variety of tables throughout the reception hall: one for the cake, one for the guest book, another for displaying pictures, and one for the gifts. This cake table holds the cake, as well as a variety of votive candles and a beautiful display of red rose petals.*

TOP LEFT: *When ordering flowers, don't forget to consider a toss bouquet, which is usually fairly simple and smaller than the bouquets carried by the bride and her attendants. The colorful toss bouquet pictured here is full of red, yellow, and pink wildflowers and tied with a pink ribbon.* TOP RIGHT: *Small bags full of pink-edged rose petals are displayed on a table and ready for guests to toss at the happy couple as they make their escape.* BOTTOM: *Ask someone to create a fun sign or simple decoration to attach to your "getaway" vehicle. Consider hiring a horse-drawn carriage to take you and your groom to a hotel or on a nice ride through the city at the end of the party.*

are bridesmaids in the line, they follow the bride and groom.

There is a trend today toward eliminating bridesmaids and groomsmen from the receiving line. Many wedding lines consist only of the bride and groom and their parents. In these cases, the other attendants are still part of the wedding party but are free to relax and visit with guests throughout the evening. In this configuration, the bride's parents often start the receiving line, followed by the bride and groom, who are then followed by the groom's parents.

In some cases, the parents of the bride and groom also prefer to circulate throughout the evening. However, it is important for the bride and groom to stay in one location so that all the guests have a chance to personally offer their congratulations.

Long conversations are out of place in a receiving line; they cause delays and are inconsiderate to the other guests who are waiting to pay their respects. Offer a simple "Thank you for coming," or a hug and kiss in this setting. Likewise, formal photographs of the wedding line should be taken before the reception begins, not while guests are waiting.

THE GETAWAY

Although in the past brides wore elegant dresses or suits with matching hats and gloves as part of their "getaway" outfit, that tradition is no longer observed. What to wear when you leave your reception has more to do with how you want to look, whether you are comfortable, and where you are going after. You might dress differently if you will be in the car for a long ride before you reach your wedding night destination than if your room is in the same hotel as your reception. Wear what makes sense to you, but avoid going too grubby. Many brides still dress smartly to depart from their receptions, and the occasional romantic even chooses to be whisked away in her wedding gown.

What to drive away in is also part of the planning for some couples. Some grooms borrow or rent classic or fancy sports cars just for the wedding night. Or this might be the time to splurge on a ride in a limousine. A romantic horse-and-buggy ride to your hotel might also be hard to resist.

The tradition of a send-off by family and loved ones can be a lovely finishing touch to your reception. Many couples have flower petals, confetti, rice, or birdseed scattered in their path as they leave. An elaborate version of this event is to release live butterflies at the couple's departure. There are companies who specialize in this, and boxed butterflies can be ordered and flown in for your wedding day, then carefully distributed to each of the guests who are to participate in your send-off festivities. White doves, which have been trained to fly home, can also be released. For more ideas on send-off activities, see the chapter on Favors.

Whatever you choose, take a moment to thank and hug those loved ones that have done so much for you— then you're off to the beginning of your new life.

This simple three-layer cake is decorated with pale pink and white frosting flowers and topped with a gold ribbon. The window in the background lets in beautiful filtered light that adds interest and depth to the cake table at this home reception.

TIPS FOR HOME RECEPTIONS

- Employ a cleaning crew before and after the wedding reception.

- Install dimmers for atmospheric lighting.

- Test all electrical lighting, as well as candles for burn times and drafts, before the reception.

- Inform neighbors of the event and make adequate arrangements for parking.

- Don't skimp on food. Having leftovers is much better than running out.

- Make sure bathrooms are accessible.

- For summer weddings, make sure you have air conditioning or an adequate cooling system. Remember that many guests in a home at the same time can raise the temperature significantly.

- In cooler weather, provide a place for guests' coats.

- Consider placing torches or luminaries leading to the entrance of the reception.

- Send out a map or directions with the invitation.

- Hire help for a home wedding, even if the number of guests in attendance is manageable. Parents and siblings should not be stuck in the kitchen; a marriage is a family affair and they deserve to enjoy the day.

- Avoid the last minute rush. Plan everything in advance.

If you are holding a wedding dinner, breakfast, or luncheon at home, be sure to pay attention to all the planning details, including the choice of silver and stemware.

TIPS FOR OUTDOOR RECEPTIONS

- Always plan an indoor backup location in case of inclement weather.

- Add trellises, gazebos, archways, or footbridges that enhance the natural beauty of the garden setting.

- Consider setting up a tent or canopy.

- Rent an elaborate water fountain for the occasion.

- Use citronella candles, or candles scented with rosemary or lemon, to help keep away insects.

- Light the evening with votive candles, lanterns, torches, or strings of white lights to add romance and ambiance to your setting.

- Plan ahead and plant flowerbeds that match the wedding colors.

- Decorate with fresh cut and potted flowers. Fresh or silk garlands are beautiful along railings, fences, and doorways.

- Choose food that will keep well out-of-doors.

- Hire a gardening crew in advance of the wedding.

- Display the wedding cake in a spot with partial or complete shade. Fondant or marzipan frosting on wedding cakes is a better choice for outdoor weddings than buttercream frosting or filled cakes.

- Plan your outdoor reception for the evening rather than the heat of the day.

TOP: *On a beautiful day, sometimes the only decoration needed at an outdoor wedding is a basket of flowers and the bride. Backyard receptions can be casual, relaxing, and fun for all involved.* BOTTOM: *This beautiful arbor at the Lion House is the perfect setting for a bridal portrait.*

When choosing an outdoor setting,
look for existing elements that could
be incorporated into your decorating:
a stone birdbath, a wreath, flowers
in hanging baskets, or your own
backyard garden, for example.

Flowers

From orange blossoms adorning the bride's hair to rose petals scattered in the couple's path, flowers are intimately connected to the romance of weddings. The flowers you choose will play a big part in the style of your wedding, so carefully to select flowers that reflect the style you wish to portray. For a French country wedding, wildflowers loosely gathered would make the perfect choice. Nosegays of red roses with the stems tightly wrapped in black silk ribbon would complement a formal wedding setting. Flowers are the element in a wedding that ties everything together, from the centerpiece on a serving table, to the tiny wedding favor, to the bride herself. When choosing the flowers for your wedding you should not only keep in mind the style you wish to create but also the season, the cost, and of course your favorite flowers.

FLORIST

You will most likely want a professional florist to create your bridal bouquet and the other flowers for your wedding. If you do not already have a favorite florist, pick one who specializes in weddings. Shop around and ask to see pictures of their arrangements. Many florists keep photographs on hand to give ideas of what you might want for your wedding and to show examples of the different styles of arrangements they have made. Find a florist who arranges flowers according to your tastes. If you love what she's done for other weddings, chances are there won't be any disappointments on your own wedding day.

COST

With modern greenhouses and overnight shipping, you can have almost any flower you want for your wedding at any time of the year. If you are trying to keep costs down, however, it is always less expensive to use flowers that are in season. For example, both lilies of the valley and lilacs are a good choice in May—at other times of the year they will cost four to five times as much. There is as wide a range in costs for flowers as there are types of flowers to choose from. Chrysanthemums, stock, freesia, snapdragons, and cosmos are inexpensive flowers, while orchids, hydrangea, and delphiniums can be quite costly.

The size of bouquets you select, the number of people in your wedding party, and whether you or the reception center are responsible for the centerpieces will also play a big part in the cost of flowers for your wedding.

SILK FLOWERS

Some brides choose silk flowers, though this is not as popular as it was in the recent past. Silk flowers may or may not be as expensive as real flowers depending on what you choose. Advantages of silk flowers are that they are easier to make ahead of time, they transport well, and are easily preserved (they stay pretty much the same as they were on your wedding day, except for possible fading and needing to be cleaned from dust).

Another thing to consider is if the bride or groom has serious allergies to fresh flowers. If the allergy is to a particular flower, it of course should be avoided. If there are problems with fresh flowers in general, silk flowers might be an appealing alternative.

But most wedding experts agree that silk flowers lack the fragrance, the romance, and the ability to capture the fleeting beauty of your wedding day.

BRIDAL BOUQUET

The bridal bouquet is central to your flowers. In fact, after your wedding gown, it is probably the most exquisite element of your reception's look and feel. The bridesmaids' bouquets, the boutonnières, centerpieces, and all other floral decorations should complement your bouquet. Your bridal bouquet will be the most important flowers you will ever carry. They should reflect you—your style, your tastes, and the gown you will wear. Decide on a few signature blooms for your bouquet, use them in abundance, and express your personality in the language of flowers.

Flowers with Meaning

Many brides choose flowers that have special significance to them. Perhaps your fiancé gave you tiny pink carnations on your first date, or you shared a glorious afternoon in the park picking violets. Memories such as these can be woven into your wedding day by incorporating the flowers associated with them into your bouquet. A touch of nostalgia can be achieved by choosing flowers in honor of special people in your life, such as a bouquet containing gardenias and peonies, the favorite flowers of each of your grandmothers. Brides in Victorian times often selected flowers by the meanings associated with them. For example, a white lily means innocence and an orchid means ecstasy.

Fragrance

Some of the most fragrant flowers include roses, gardenias, stephanotis, Casablanca and stargazer lilies, freesia, and sweet peas. These blooms might be mixed

French garden roses, full pink ranunculus, pale pink snapdragons, and bunches of white hydrangea make a beautiful spring bouquet. A wicker basket of rose petals, an elegant boutonnière made of white hydrangea and dainty winterberries, and a delicate floral headpiece all complement the charming cascade bouquet.

This unique, contemporary bouquet, with subtle hints of white, green, and brown, is made of stargazer lilies, white dendrobium orchids, brown millett, and fern curls.

with other less fragrant flowers to achieve the perfect bouquet. Homegrown lilacs are very fragrant but extremely fragile; while the more hearty hothouse variety have no aroma at all.

Style and Size

Bridal bouquets can be designed in many ways. Standard styles include nosegay, globe, cascade, and gathered. Ask your florist to see examples of the different styles of arrangements to see what your preferences are.

Bridal bouquets must match your wedding dress. If you've chosen an airy organza gown, cascades of ruffled tulips and Canterbury bells or delicate Queen Anne's lace might be the perfect choice. A sleek modern gown would lend itself to a sheath of calla lilies or a single perfect rose.

Flowers should not overwhelm the dress or the bride herself. Bouquets should be proportionate to the woman's height and weight, the fullness of her skirt and the length of her train. Brides should also consider the length of time they will be holding the flowers; some arrangements take only one hand, others are heavy and large enough to require both hands most of the time. Of course, a petite bride can carry a large bouquet, but it should not be so big as to draw more attention to the flowers than to the bride herself.

Season and Color

In addition to picking your favorite flowers, the season you have chosen for your wedding is extremely important in selecting flowers. The color theme for your

Roses, which come in many styles and colors, are often the flowers of choice for the bridal bouquet. And even though "a rose is a rose is a rose," this doesn't mean that all rose bouquets are alike. LEFT: This elegant dome bouquet is a romantic gathering of creamy, full roses tied with a large satin ribbon. RIGHT: Dozens of tight white and yellow rosebuds, mixed with purple statice and green ivy leaves create this formal cascade bouquet.

wedding is also crucial, and wedding colors are often selected to match the season.

For a spring bouquet you might choose a bunch of white and pink tulips punctuated with lilies of the valley. Delicate crocus or grape hyacinths also make excellent springtime bouquets. Consider incorporating branches of fresh cherry blossoms into arrangements. Wild looking poppies are lovely but extremely fragile and do not hold up well.

In summer a bride might pick a bunch of cheerful daisies tied with ribbon or a grouping of fragrant sweet peas—lavender, salmon, pale pink, or dark purple. A spray of freesia and lilies also makes an excellent choice. A summer bride might also choose a bouquet including fresh herbs, such as lavender or blossoming chives.

A fall bouquet might be a combination of rich red roses and burnt orange chrysanthemums. You might choose a dome of orange roses or a formally grouped nosegay of dahlias. Wild sunflowers also make beautiful autumn bouquets.

Winter bouquets might be red roses and snowberries, a collared bouquet of gardenias, or simply a sheath of rich dark greenery.

A Word on Whites

The longstanding favorite color for bridal bouquets is white. Although white itself is a very classic color, white flowers can be combined into bouquets of many different styles. White roses with stephanotis have a traditional feel, while white gardenias are more elegant. White orchids can be exotic, white calla lilies chic, and an armful of white ranunculus and snapdragons appealingly informal.

LEFT: A summer garden wedding may call for a bouquet as simple as a few pink daisies tied with a silky ribbon. RIGHT: White lilies and tiny paperwhites are touched with a douse of pink roses and lavender freesia.

TOP LEFT: *This bouquet draws from the splendor of old-fashioned white roses, simple white stock, and inexpensive cushion mums.* TOP MIDDLE: *A vase of white tulips makes a thoughtful centerpiece at a casual wedding.* TOP RIGHT: *This casual bouquet of white spray roses, lisianthus, and stock is touched with color from tiny waxflowers.* BOTTOM: *This elegant, all-white bouquet is a mix of akito roses and stephanotis with petite pearl centers. The hand-tied bouquet is accented with plumosa fern, lemon leaves, Israel ruskus, and looped bear grass.*

In this Christmas-themed bouquet, red roses and hydrangea are set atop a few sprigs of cedar greenery and bunches of pepper berries. The stems are tightly wrapped in a silky, cream-colored cord.

Florists agree that although there are a multitude of shades of white—from bright white to eggshell to bisque to pink-tinged whites to creamy yellows to those touched with green—almost any combination of white flowers will blend together beautifully. If you desire a white bouquet that exactly matches the color of your gown, you will need to take a matching swatch of fabric with you to your florist.

White bouquets have the advantage of being as beautiful in the winter as they are in the summertime.

A Word on Roses

Roses are a perfect choice for any season. Associated with love, passion, and romance, they are also the favorite choice of almost every bride, whether used alone or grouped with other flowers. In choosing roses, do not overlook the wide range of colors and types available. They come in every imaginable hue of red, pink, white, yellow, cream, peach, orange, and even in lavender and green. Tropical roses with huge blooms, tea roses, and old-fashioned roses will all give a different feel. Fully opened roses can be used as beautifully as barely opening buds. Some bouquets use a combination of roses at different stages of opening to achieve the desired effect. Roses have a lovely fragrance and an ability to last after they are cut that will make them an enjoyable flower to hold throughout the evening.

The flowers you choose for your bridal bouquet should be echoed in the bridesmaids' bouquets, as well as the boutonnières for the men and the corsages for the mothers. Flowers for centerpieces and other decorations should also match what you have chosen.

Roses are a romantic choice for any floral display. ABOVE, FROM LEFT: Petite garden spray roses; perfectly formed peach roses from your favorite florist; or dramatic, fully opened pink blooms touched with shades of white are only a few examples of the wide range of colors and types available.

*This cascade of stargazer lilies, yellow
freesia, pink rosebuds, purple irises,
alstroemeria, and heather is perfect for the
bride who wants something different from
the traditional rose bouquet. Eucalyptus
leaves, bear grass, and Italian ruskus
make a nice finishing touch.*

TOP LEFT: *This bright yellow bouquet—a combination of vibrant roses, Asiatic lilies, button chrysanthemums, golden aster, and variegated pittosporum—is perfect for summer.* TOP RIGHT: *This pastel bouquet—made from white roses, lisianthus, pink and white carnations, freesia, and bella donna delphinium—is both pretty and economical because it relies on greenery and inexpensive flowers to fill out the arrangement.* BOTTOM LEFT: *Light pink tulips, yellow roses, blue hydrangea, pink sweet peas, and white stephanotis create a sweet and fragrant spring bouquet.* BOTTOM RIGHT: *This red and pink cascade bouquet would be perfect for a Valentine's Day bride. Red, white, and pink roses are accented with pink freesia; and rich red heather adds height to the bouquet.*

BOUTONNIÈRES

Boutonnières for the men are one of those finishing touches of a wedding that tie everything together and make it complete. The groom, fathers of the bride and groom, and any of the groom's attendants should wear boutonnières. Sometimes the groom honors the grandfathers with boutonnières as well.

The groom's boutonnière should contain flowers that look as though they have been plucked from the bride's bouquet. It should also be distinguished from the others by being slightly larger or including different blooms or greenery. However, be careful of the common mistake of making the groom's boutonnière too large. You do not want it to look like he is wearing a corsage. Small and sleek boutonnières are the best.

A traditional rosebud is nice, but you may want to investigate other possibilities. Tiny lilies of the valley, a stem of freesia, a simple cosmo, or stephanotis supported with a pearl-headed pin all make beautiful boutonnières. Other options besides flowers also make excellent choices, such as sprigs of fresh herbs, greenery, or fall or winter berries.

BRIDESMAIDS' BOUQUETS

Some brides have a long formal receiving line with several attendants; others have bridesmaids who carry flowers, but rather than standing in line mingle with guests throughout the evening. Still other brides choose only one maid or matron of honor, or have no bridesmaids at all. Whatever you choose for your wedding,

bridal attendants should hold flowers that complement the bridal bouquet.

Bridesmaids' bouquets may be a scaled down version of the bridal bouquet itself, or simply a repetition of one of the flowers in the bridal bouquet. For example, a bride carrying a bouquet of hydrangeas and sweet peas may provide her attendants with simple nosegays comprised of sweet peas only. Or bridesmaids may carry a single bloom represented in the bridal bouquet, such as a calla lily or a rose. A Casablanca lily or iris would probably not be good choices, since irises wilt quickly and the Casablanca lily can easily stain the bridesmaid's dress.

In most cases, bridesmaids' bouquets should be identical to each other. However, for a more informal wedding, as long as the flowers of each bridesmaid complement each other and tie in with the rest of the wedding flowers, you can stray from the traditional a little on this point.

CORSAGES

Corsages for the mothers of the bride and groom are a nice way to honor these important members of your wedding party. The flowers selected should reflect the bridal bouquet. Sometimes brides choose to honor the grandmothers, or a special aunt, with corsages as well.

FLOWER GIRLS

The beauty and innocence of a flower girl often creates a cherished image from the wedding day. Wearing dresses of satin, starched cotton, or organza, flower girls

OPPOSITE: Boutonnières can be made from practically any type of flower as long as they match the bridal bouquet. TOP LEFT: A single white rose and two small stephanotis with pearl centers. TOP MIDDLE: A sprig of hypericum. TOP RIGHT: A peach rose accented with bupleurum. CLOCKWISE FROM LEFT: Lush hot pink cockscomb, with purple freesia, larkspur, and hypericum berries; A full lavender rose bloom flanked by heather, bella donna delphinium, and yellow button mums; A dendrobium orchid with a fern curl; A single red rose, delicate pepper berries, and a touch of hydrangea.

TOP: A single calla lily is the focus of this beautiful centerpiece of creamy green and white tuber roses. BOTTOM: This jewel-toned bouquet complements the centerpiece to the right and is made of gloriosa lilies, red and purple freesia, terra-cotta roses, purple lisianthus, hypericum, and seeded eucalyptus, all tied tight with a wide, sheer ribbon.

are often adorned with rings of flowers on their heads, from an elegant crown of pale roses to a sprightly ring of intertwined daisies or wildflowers. They usually carry baskets filled with petals for them to scatter in front of the bride and groom. The basket can be a traditional handheld woven basket decorated with fresh flowers, or a basket covered in satin or filmy gauze. Rose petals matching the colors of the wedding are a favorite choice for petals to be strewn in the path of the couple or tossed at them as they depart for their honeymoon.

CENTERPIECES

Many reception centers provide centerpieces for their tables and often have several to choose from. If this is the case for your wedding, choose the center-piece that most closely matches the style and theme of your wedding.

In cases where you will be providing the flowers for your tables, remember to reflect the style of your bridal bouquet, though you do not need to duplicate it exactly. One option is to choose the largest or the most inexpensive flower from your bouquet to feature in centerpiece arrangements. Typically centerpieces should be identical for each table, though there may be occasions where this is not the case. For example, if the bride carries a bouquet of red, orange, and peach roses, each centerpiece could feature roses of all one color: one table with red roses, one table with orange roses, and so on.

Remember when creating centerpieces not to make arrangements so large that there is not enough room for guests to place their food to eat comfortably. Also be especially careful not to create centerpieces that are so tall that people cannot see each other or converse

This gorgeous centerpiece uses bunches of
tiny champagne grapes, red pomegranates,
and tiny key limes in combination with
lush red and orange roses, rich cockscomb,
purple irises, vibrant gloriosa lilies, and
small round pepper berries.

comfortably over them. The centerpiece should be in proportion to the table and enhance the experience of the guest, not detract from it. A larger centerpiece is often made for the serving table if you are having a buffet.

Since you will not want twelve or more fresh floral centerpieces after the wedding is over, a pleasant bonus of providing your own centerpieces is that you have a lovely gift for family or friends to take home and enjoy.

Your florist will be experienced in creating arrangements for weddings and can offer good suggestions on the best choices for your centerpieces and other flowers you will use to decorate for your reception.

OTHER FLOWERS

Brides must not overlook a flower arrangement for their book-signing table. These are often the first flowers guests see when they arrive at the reception and will give them an idea of the style and theme of the wedding.

An alternative for wedding breakfast or formal dinner tables is tying a bunch of flowers to the backs of the guests' chairs rather than using centerpieces. This makes an unusual and beautifully decorated table and leaves the center of the table open for serving and passing the food.

If you are giving flowers as wedding favors, you will want to coordinate this with the other flowers you are using for your wedding. Ideally, potted pansies, tiny bud vases of freesia, fresh lavender in sachets, or boxed rose petals should match the style and types of flowers used for the rest of the wedding, from the centerpieces to the bridal bouquet.

Flowers can be used throughout your reception. LEFT: These tiered arrangements use a variety of spring flowers and look beautiful at a buffet table. RIGHT: These three fondant-draped cakes are topped with a combination of white roses, posy calla lilies, freesia, and maple vine.

Flower Guide

FLOWER	SEASON	COLOR	PRICE RANGE
Amaryllis	winter	red, white, reddish orange, pink, variegated	medium
Anemone	spring	red, pink, white, purple	low
Anthurium	year round	red, pink, white	medium
Bird of Paradise	winter	orange	high
Bleeding Heart	summer	pink, lavender	low
Cherry Blossoms	spring	hot pink, soft pink	medium
Daffodil	spring	yellow	low
Dahlia	fall	pink, lavender, red, yellow, white, bronze, plumb, bicolor	low
Delphinium	year round	dark blue, light blue, white	low
Freesia	year round	purple, lavender, yellow, hot pink, white	low
Gardenia	year round	white	high
Gerbera Daisy	year round	shades of yellow, orange, red, peach, pink, white	low
Gloriosa Lily	fall	hot pink with bright yellow tips	medium
Gomphrena	fall	pink, lavender, bright purple	low
Hyacinth	spring	pink, white, purple	medium
Hydrangea	summer	pink, blue, green, burgundy, light blue	high
Iris	year round	yellow, blue, purple	low
Larkspur	year round	pink, purple, white	low
Liatris	year round	purple, white	low
Lily of the Valley	spring	white	high
Lisianthus	year round	purple, soft yellow, lavender, pink	medium
Orchid	year round	purple, white, yellow	high
Peonies	spring	hot pink, pink, white, red	high
Posy Callas	year round	pink, ivory, eggplant plumb, flame orange, white	high
Ranunculus	spring	pink, white, hot pink, red, yellow, orange	low
Rose	year round	shades of white, cream, yellow, red, peach, orange, brown, and lavender, bicolor	medium
Snapdragon	year round	yellow, orange, burgundy, white, pink	low
Spray Roses	year round	pink, red, yellow, orange	medium
Stargazer Lily	year round	burgundy white tips and white	high
Stephanotis	year round	white	low
Stock	year round	purple, white, lavender, yellow, peach	low
Sunflower	summer	yellow	low
Sweet Pea	spring	peach, pink, lavender, white	low
Tuberose	year round	creamy white	low
Tulip	spring	pink, purple, white, yellow, red, orange	medium
Winterberry	winter	white, soft pink	medium

Pricing is subject to change due to availability and season. Holiday prices will be inflated.

Anemone

Anthurium

Aster

Azalea

Begonia

Bird of Paradise

Bleeding Heart

Camellia

Campanula

Carnation

Chrysanthemum

Columbine

Cornflower

Cranesbill

Daffodil

Dahlia

Daisy

Day Lily

Dendrobium Orchid

Easter Lily

Freesia

Gardenia

Gerbera Daisy

Gladiola

Godetia

Hyacinth (blossom)

Hydrangea

Impatiens

Kalanchoe

Lily

Lily of the Valley

Magnolia

Morning Glory

Orchid

Pansy

Poppy

Primrose

Primula

Ranunculus

Rose

Rose

Snapdragon

Spider Mum

Stargazer Lily

Sunflower

Sweet Pea

Trillium

Tulip

Food

Few things set the tone of your wedding more than the food you choose to serve. Whether it is filet mignon with crab claws at a formal dinner, muffins and ripe melons at a wedding breakfast, or an icy berry frappe at a garden reception, your food adds a rich layer of romance and sensuality to your celebration. The intimacy created by sharing food together is nowhere more noticeable than at a wedding.

When planning the food for your wedding there are several things you will want to consider. First you will need to determine the event—whether it is a wedding breakfast, luncheon, dinner, reception, or open house. You must also consider the setting and scale of your wedding, the style, the budget, and the season.

CHOOSING THE EVENT

There are many choices for how you want to gather people together to celebrate your marriage. What is important is that you pick what works best for you.

For example, do you want a traditional wedding breakfast for family and close friends following an early morning temple ceremony? Or do you have guests and family from several different religions, where a luncheon not closely associated in time or proximity to a temple sealing would be easier for everyone? Do you want to celebrate with dinner at your favorite restaurant? Or are there many children you want to include in your wedding that would make a backyard retreat more appropriate?

Many Latter-day Saint brides, particularly along the Wasatch Front, have a large-scale wedding reception with two to five hundred guests. In this case, a well-chosen refreshment plate is often the best option, providing guests with a few tasty bites to savor rather than a full-fledged meal. Another attractive option for a large reception is a cake buffet (featuring several choices of different cakes) or a dessert buffet (featuring several

choices of desserts, such as a slice of chocolate cream cake, a strawberry tart, and a crème brûlée).

Another nice choice for couples is to avoid the fuss of a huge reception altogether and replace it instead with a more intimate gathering at a formal dinner. This dinner is for anywhere from thirty to eighty guests, and is often the night before the wedding. The cost of a big reception can be focused on a more limited number of guests, giving you more freedom with fancy menus. This is a good choice for couples who prefer a smaller setting to a large-scale celebration. It is also an ideal solution for couples who are marrying for the second time or if they are blending families with their marriage. It allows them to celebrate the importance and joy of the event without the complexities involved in a reception.

The parents of the groom may wish to host an open house in addition to the bride and groom's wedding reception. This is often the case when the bride and groom's families live in different cities. An open house is more casual than a reception, with a shorter guest list. As the name "open house" suggests, it is often hosted in the family home of the groom. It is usually given a week or two after the wedding. Food for an open house would be along the lines of a smaller refreshment plate or dessert buffet.

DECIDING SETTING, SCALE, AND STYLE

The place you hold your wedding breakfast, dinner, or reception will depend on a number of factors, from what kind of event it is, to how many people you want

ABOVE LEFT: Receptions or other wedding events can take on a number of different looks. This hall is set up so that guests seat themselves at the table of their choice and await service of a simple refreshment plate. ABOVE RIGHT: Dinner guests at the Joseph Smith Memorial Building can serve themselves at a grand buffet.

to invite, to how much money you want to spend. You should consider all your options and pick a setting and a scale for your event that is most appropriate for you. Some people choose to have fewer guests and a more expensive offering; others want to share their celebration with everyone and a slice of cake will do.

Where you decide to hold your event will have an impact on the food you decide to serve. Will it be indoors or out? Will you be eating at a reception center, church, or historic building, at a poolside, golf course, or mountain retreat? Does your setting lend itself to cold or hot food, to food that can be prepared in advance, to catered food, to a buffet or a sit-down meal?

If, for example, you choose a traditional wedding at a reception center, you might serve tiny ham sandwiches with fresh vegetables and dip. For the most for-

mal occasion, a large-scale buffet with several meats, breads, vegetable dishes, salads, and a variety of desserts might be served. An outdoor reception might lend itself to fruit kabobs, cookies, and clever sandwich wraps, while a wedding breakfast at the Lion House or Joseph Smith Memorial Building would offer many different menu choices for plated meals.

The style of your wedding will also determine in large part what you serve. For example, your food choices will be much different if you have an elegant black-tie affair than if you choose a backyard reception or a gathering at the beach. A Hawaiian-themed wedding has obvious menu choices, as does a family barbeque. If you want dinner at your favorite Italian restaurant you will be inviting fewer people than if you rent a reception center. If you decide you want a formal dinner

LEFT: When setting tables for a dinner or luncheon, be sure to coordinate everything from the linens to the food. Here, pink punch, a light pink ribbon around the tablecloth, and a delicate spring centerpiece all unite for a lovely presentation. RIGHT: Tall silver-plated cylinders hold elegant arrangements of white lilies, tulips, roses, and hyacinths, adding interest to this buffet table.

TOP: Refreshment plates can be as simple as a cookie or as elegant as this hot creamed chicken served in a puff pastry alongside melon slices and berries. BOTTOM: For a wedding luncheon, ham with pineapple sauce, au gratin potatoes, and fresh green beans make an excellent menu. The meal is served here with chocolate silk pie for dessert.

the night before the wedding, you should do that instead of a wedding breakfast after the ceremony—don't do both. Think through your options and choose the setting, scale, and style for your wedding celebration that appeals to you.

RECOGNIZING YOUR BUDGET

There are few people who have an unlimited amount of money to spend on their wedding. Recognizing the realities of your budget is important as you plan your events. But remember that you need not have a great deal of money to have good taste. You can make wise choices for your food on both a large and a small budget. French vanilla ice cream with a few fresh boysenberries can fit the mood of your wedding as nicely as a grand buffet with shrimp and prime rib. After deciding on the style of wedding you want and the guest list, you can make a tasteful menu on almost any budget.

GLORYING IN THE SEASON

Choose a variety of food to match the style of your wedding and the season. Fresh fruit is always much less expensive and more flavorful when it is in season. Strawberries may be available in January, but are less flavorful and more expensive than they will be in June. Keep in mind that fresh melons, mangos, and berries might not be the wisest winter menu. Instead, select flavors and foods that match what nature is doing at the time of year you are married.

Fall suggests warm ciders, spicy pumpkin breads, and rich fruits, like an apple and blueberry cobbler or baked pears. Guests appreciate hearty soups and heavy breads much more now than they would in summer. Homemade pies make an excellent dessert at this time of year.

Christmas or winter weddings might suggest a hot wassail, rich cheesecake, and desserts with puddings and warm sauces. Cranberry drinks or snowflake sugar cookies tie in the season with your wedding. Main courses might be roast beef or slow-roasted turkey breast.

Summer is the time for fresh fruits and melons, cascades of grapes, and bowls of raspberries with cream. Cold sherbets and frappes are refreshingly cool at this time of year. Chocolate-dipped strawberries or homemade ice cream make perfect summer refreshments. Cakes should be light, such as a fluffy angel food cake, rather than a heavy spice cake. Pasta dishes or cold sandwiches are appealing in summer.

Spring offers a wider variety of choices for your menu than any other time of year. Desserts of every kind are an option, and some fruits may be in season. Salads are always a pleasant complement to a meal, and many salads can serve as the meal itself when accompanied by good bread. Chicken salad on a croissant or a warm spinach salad with salmon would make excellent choices for a wedding luncheon.

SELECTING A MENU

If you are having your wedding at a reception center, the Lion House, or the Joseph Smith Building, their staff will assist you in deciding on the menu you will serve, whether it is for a breakfast, luncheon, dinner, or reception. Check with your reception center regarding the food at the time of booking. You will need to discuss prices, menus, and the number of guests you will be serving. Most often reception centers will provide the food themselves (usually at an additional cost to renting the facility) or have a list of preferred caterers. Most reception centers will not allow you to bring in your own food.

In cases and settings where you will be making your own food for the wedding, a detailed listing of menus and recipes is included in this chapter. Whether you are giving a reception indoors or out-of-doors, hosting an open house, or offering an elegant sit-down dinner for the families of the bride and groom, you can select one of the predetermined menus provided or choose from the dozens of recipes to create your own perfect menu. Many of the menus and recipes could easily be adapted for a bridal shower as well. You can follow the menus as they are presented, mix and match menus, or use them as a springboard for your own ideas and favorite recipes.

Wedding Breakfasts

Wedding breakfasts are typically held between 8 A.M. and noon. Menus for breakfasts often include traditional, though elegantly presented items, such as muffins or a Danish, hashbrowns or potatoes O'Brien, ham or sausage, French toast or omelets. They include more formal offerings as well, such as scrambled eggs in a phyllo cup or a fruit and yogurt parfait.

Ham Quiche

3 9-inch frozen pie shells
1 quart half-and-half
9 eggs
1 teaspoon salt
½ teaspoon white pepper
2 teaspoons fresh parsley, chopped
1 teaspoon fresh thyme, chopped
2¼ cups (½ pound) cheddar cheese, shredded
2¼ cups (½ pound) Swiss cheese, shredded
1 cup ham, diced

Preheat oven to 350° F. Place the pie shells on an ovenproof baking sheet. Bake in the oven for 5 minutes or until the shells are just turning golden brown.

While the shells are baking, mix the half-and-half, eggs, salt, white pepper, parsley, and thyme in a large bowl. Stir for 1 minute to dissolve salt.

In another bowl mix the cheeses and ham. Once the shells are cooked, remove them from the oven and fill each with a third of the cheese and ham mixture. Pour one-third of the egg mixture into each shell.

Place the quiche on baking sheets and set them in the oven. Reduce oven temperature to 275° F. and bake for 40 minutes. When slightly shaken, the quiche should not seem fluid. Remove from oven and let sit for 5 minutes to set the custard. Cut each into 8 pieces and serve. Makes 24 servings.

Scrambled Eggs in a Phyllo Cup

1 package phyllo dough, thawed
½ cup clarified butter
40 eggs
1 teaspoon salt
½ teaspoon white pepper
1 teaspoon fresh thyme, chopped
1 teaspoon fresh parsley, chopped
1 teaspoon fresh rosemary, chopped

Preheat oven to 350° F. Unroll the phyllo dough onto a clean work surface. Take a sharp knife and cut lengthwise across the center of the sheets. Then make two cuts from top to bottom, cutting the dough into 6 equal rectangles approximately 4x4½ inches.

Take one of these sheets and lay it on a clean portion of your work surface. Using a clean pastry brush, brush a small amount of clarified butter over this sheet. Take another sheet of dough and lay it across the first sheet, making a "T." Brush a small amount of clarified butter over this sheet. Take another sheet of dough and lay it across the first two. Carefully lift the dough into one of the muffin cups in a muffin tin. Press down the center, leaving the sheets hanging over the edges. Continue filling the muffin pan until you have filled all the holes. The dough may overlap a bit. This will not harm the final product.

Bake in preheated oven for 5 minutes, or until the cups are light golden brown. Watch the time carefully, as the cups can burn easily. When done, remove pan from oven and let cool. Remove each cup one at a time, beginning with the last cup to be put into the pan. Repeat the above steps until you have enough cups for your number of guests. Store these uncovered until service.

Half an hour before service, break the eggs into a large bowl, add the salt and pepper, and beat with a whisk. Pour the egg mixture into a large nonstick skillet or cook in small batches until the eggs are completely cooked. Add the fresh herbs to the eggs and mix to evenly distribute. When you are ready to serve, place the phyllo cup onto a plate and spoon in enough eggs to fill the cup.

Serve the eggs immediately. Holding the eggs at this point will make the phyllo soggy. Makes 20 servings.

Southwest Egg Wrap with Homemade Salsa

20 jalapeño flavored tortillas

40 eggs

½ teaspoon salt

¼ teaspoon white pepper

3 tablespoons olive oil

2 red peppers, julienned

2 green peppers, julienned

2 yellow peppers, julienned

2 red onions, julienned

40 slices bacon, cooked and drained

5 cups (1¼ pounds) cheddar cheese, shredded

5 tomatoes, diced

1 recipe Fruit Salsa

Beat eggs and season with salt and pepper. Cover and store this in the refrigerator until ready for service.

Preheat a sauté pan until a small amount of water sizzles in the pan. Carefully add the olive oil to coat the bottom of the pan. Add the peppers and onions to the hot pan. Sauté these only until the color of the peppers brightens slightly. Do not overcook them. Set these aside and keep warm.

Scramble the eggs in another hot sauté or nonstick pan. When you are ready to make the wraps, place a warmed tortilla in the center of a clean work area. Spoon in ½ cup of scrambled eggs, two strips of bacon, and 2 tablespoons of the pepper and onion mixture. Add approximately ¼ cup of the shredded cheddar cheese. Fold up the tortilla from the bottom, bringing the bottom two-thirds of the way up the center. Fold in each side approximately 1 inch. Roll the wrap up to complete the fold and set aside—keeping it warm—until you complete all the wraps.

Serve the wrap whole or cut in half on a plate with Fruit Salsa (see page 64) as a garnish. Makes 20 wraps.

TOP: Southwest egg wraps with homemade salsa add a bit of spicy flavor to any wedding breakfast. BOTTOM: Wedding breakfasts can be dressed-up offerings or simple fare. Scrambled eggs in a phyllo cup make an elegant statement.

Fruit Salsa

1 cantaloupe, peeled and diced

1 honeydew melon, peeled and diced

1 red onion, peeled and diced

1 red bell pepper, diced

1 yellow bell pepper, diced

2 tablespoons fresh cilantro, chopped

2 tablespoons lime juice

1 jalapeño chili pepper

3 tablespoons raspberry vinegar

½ teaspoon salt

3 tablespoons olive oil

Combine all ingredients in a glass bowl. Cover and refrigerate for at least 1 hour. Makes 20 two-ounce servings.

Eggs Benedict

20 English muffins

40 slices Canadian bacon

40 poached eggs

1 recipe Hollandaise Sauce

Split the English muffins in half and arrange each on a plate. Place one slice of Canadian bacon on each half of the muffin. Carefully spoon the poached eggs onto the Canadian bacon. Pour one ounce of sauce onto each egg. Serve immediately. Makes 20 servings.

Poached Eggs

1 quart water

1 teaspoon salt

1 teaspoon white vinegar

40 whole eggs

Fill a large opened pot with the water, salt, and vinegar. Bring the water temperature to 200° F. Break the eggs into small individual cups.

Slowly slide the eggs out of the cups into the hot water. Cook them for 3 to 4 minutes or until the whites have just turned white. Remove from the water with a slotted spoon. Serve immediately.

Hollandaise Sauce

¼ cup rice wine vinegar

12 egg yolks

4 teaspoons lemon juice

2 teaspoons Tabasco sauce

3 cups clarified butter, melted, warm

¾ cup water

1 teaspoon salt

Combine the vinegar, egg yolks, lemon juice, and Tabasco sauce in a stainless steel bowl. Whip this mixture over simmering water until the yolks become light yellow in color. Care should be taken at this point. Overcooking the eggs is easy to do. If the eggs begin to scramble, remove the bowl from the simmering water and whisk briskly to break up the bits of egg. If the eggs scramble too much, you must start over. Gradually add the clarified butter, drizzling it into the egg mixture. Add the water slowly to thin the sauce to a pourable consistency. Finish the sauce with the salt. Hollandaise should be served warm. Makes 20 servings.

Note: Making Hollandaise sauce befuddles some of the best cooks. If you watch carefully as you are whisking the eggs over the simmering water—removing the bowl when the eggs get too hot and replacing it when they have cooled again—you will not scramble the eggs. Also, when adding the clarified butter, be sure to very slowly drizzle it into the eggs, whisking constantly as you emulsify the sauce.

French Toast Triangles

40 slices Texas Toast style bread, day old

5 eggs, slightly beaten

1½ cups heavy cream

2 teaspoons vanilla extract

¼ cup powdered sugar

Nonstick pan spray or butter substitute

In a medium bowl, mix the eggs, cream, vanilla, and sugar. Preheat a large skillet or electric skillet. Spray the skillet with the pan spray or for more flavor use a liquid butter substitute on the pan. Quickly dredge the Texas toast slices in the egg mixture and set them on the skillet.

Cook over medium heat until golden brown, turn and cook the second side. Cut each slice in half diagonally. Hold finished French toast in a warm oven until ready to serve. Sprinkle with powdered sugar immediately before service. Makes 20 servings.

Note: Using slightly stale bread will make better French toast.

Hash Browned Potatoes

10 cups Idaho potatoes, peeled and diced
3 tablespoons clarified butter
3 teaspoons fresh thyme, chopped
Salt and pepper to taste

Cook the potatoes in salted boiling water for 10 minutes or until tender. Remove from heat, drain, and set aside. Heat a large skillet until a drop of water sizzles. Add the clarified butter and the potatoes. Add the fresh thyme, salt, and pepper. Cook the potatoes until they are browned on one side and then turn to brown the second side. Remove from heat and serve immediately. (Potatoes will be soggy if held.) Makes twenty ½-cup servings.

Potato Wedges

10 cups Yukon gold Idaho potatoes, peeled
3 tablespoons clarified butter
1 teaspoon salt
½ teaspoon white pepper
3 teaspoons fresh parsley, chopped

Cut the potatoes into uniform wedges. Cook the potatoes in salted boiling water for 10 minutes or until tender. Remove from heat, drain, and set aside. Heat a large skillet until a drop of water sizzles. Add the clarified butter and the potatoes. Cook the potatoes until they are browned and crisp on one side and then turn to brown the second side. Once the potatoes are cooled, remove pan from heat and toss in salt, pepper, and fresh parsley until potatoes are evenly coated. (Potatoes will be soggy if held.) Makes 20 half-cup servings.

Fruit Salad

20 cantaloupe slices
20 honeydew melon slices
20 watermelon slices
20 strawberries
1 pint raspberries
20 mint sprigs

This recipe works best with ripe, sweet fruit. If you are preparing this salad when any of the listed fruits are not available, substitutions may be made. Arrange each slice of fruit on the plate to your liking. Use strawberries, raspberries, or other berries as garnish. Finish with a sprig of mint. Serve immediately. Makes 20 sliced-fruit salads.

Fruit and Yogurt Parfait

1 quart blueberry yogurt
1 quart peach yogurt
1 quart raspberry yogurt
1 16-ounce box muselix cereal
4 cups raspberries
4 cups strawberries, quartered
4 cups blueberries
Raspberries, for garnish
Mint sprigs, for garnish

In tall parfait-style glasses alternate yogurt, muselix cereal, and berries to fill each glass. Garnish top with whole raspberries and a sprig of mint. Makes 20 parfaits.

Blueberry Muffins

3½ cups all-purpose flour
½ cup sugar
5 teaspoons baking powder
½ teaspoon salt
2 eggs, well-beaten
1½ cups milk
⅔ cup oil
2 cups fresh blueberries*

Eggs benedict and a yogurt parfait make a beautiful and unusual offering for a wedding breakfast. The yogurt parfait would also make a nice choice to serve at a bridal shower.

Sift flour, sugar, baking powder, and salt into a bowl; make a well in the center. In another bowl, beat together eggs, milk, and oil. Pour mixture into well and stir until moistened. Gently fold in blueberries.

Grease muffin tins or use baking cups. Fill each two-thirds full of batter. Bake at 400° F. for 20 to 25 minutes. Makes 20 muffins.

*Frozen blueberries may be substituted. Thaw and drain before using.

Danish Pastry

½ cup warm water
2 tablespoons yeast
1 tablespoon sugar
1 cup softened butter or margarine
2 cups warm milk
¾ cup sugar
1 teaspoon salt
2 eggs
8 cups flour
Sliced or slivered almonds
1 recipe Cream Filling
1 recipe Almond Filling
1 recipe Streusel Topping
1 recipe Almond Icing

Put ½ cup warm water in a bowl. Sprinkle yeast and 1 tablespoon sugar over water; set aside. Meanwhile, combine butter, milk, ¾ cup sugar, salt, and eggs in a large bowl. Stir in yeast mixture. Add flour and mix till well blended but do not overmix. Cover and let rise till double. Punch down. In the meantime, make Cream Filling, Almond Filling, Streusel Topping, and Almond Icing.

Directions for assembling: Divide dough into 4 equal parts. On lightly floured board, roll out each part into a rectangle. Spread one-fourth Cream Filling on each; then one-fourth Almond Filling on each. Roll up jelly-roll fashion. Cut about 10 slashes through top with knife. Place each roll on greased cookie sheet. Sprinkle with Streusel Topping. Let rise in a warm place till double in bulk. Bake at 375° F. for 20 minutes. Drizzle with Almond Icing and sprinkle with sliced or slivered almonds. Cut each into 6 pieces. Makes 24 large Danishes.

CREAM FILLING

1 cup milk
1 egg yolk
½ teaspoon salt
⅓ cup sugar
2 tablespoons flour

Heat milk in saucepan. Mix egg yolk into dry ingredients. Add a little warm milk to dry ingredients, then mix with heated milk and stir and cook till thick. Cover with plastic wrap and cool.

ALMOND FILLING

½ cup butter or margarine
¾ cup sugar
½ cup oats
2 teaspoons almond flavoring

Mix all ingredients with fork, wire whip, or mixer till well blended.

STREUSEL TOPPING

½ cup flour
½ cup sugar
¼ cup butter

Mix all ingredients with fork until small crumbs form.

ALMOND ICING

1 cup powdered sugar
2 to 3 tablespoons milk or cream
1 teaspoon almond flavoring

Combine powdered sugar with enough milk or cream to make slightly runny icing. Add almond flavoring.

Ham quiche is an excellent choice for a wedding brunch any time of year. Here it is served with a fresh fruit salad.

Wedding Luncheons

The wedding luncheon is a midday meal generally served before or after the wedding ceremony. Luncheon menus can be light, including sandwiches and fresh fruit, or they can consist of several courses and function as the main meal of the day. Swiss chicken with asparagus and a rice pilaf, as well as rolls, a salad, and a dessert would make up a more formal wedding luncheon.

Suggested Menus for Wedding Luncheons

- Bacon and Tomato Sandwich, Grapefruit and Avocado Salad

- Pork Tenderloin with Balsamic Apple Sauce, Mashed Potatoes, Steamed Broccoli, Lion House Rolls

- Apricot Cranberry Chicken Breast, Confetti Risotto, Vegetable Medley, Snowpea Cucumber Salad

- Ham with Pineapple Sauce, Au Gratin Potatoes, Fresh String Green Beans, Chocolate Silk Pie

- Swiss Chicken, Rice Pilaf, Fresh Asparagus Tips, Lion House Rolls, Pink Angel Dessert

- Beef Roulade, Baby Red Potatoes, Roasted Julienne Root Vegetables, Lemon Cheesecake

Pork Tenderloin with Balsamic Apple Sauce

PORK TENDERLOIN

7½ pounds pork tenderloin
Salt and pepper to taste
¼ cup clarified butter

Sprinkle each tenderloin with salt and pepper and set in a bowl. Heat a large sauté pan over high heat until a small amount of water dropped on the pan sizzles. Add about 2 tablespoons of the clarified butter to the hot pan. Carefully place enough tenderloins in the pan so that it is filled but not crowded. Sauté each side of the loins until they have browned. Remove from the pan and place in a shallow baking pan. Repeat the above steps until all the pork is browned.

Preheat oven to 350° F. Place the tenderloins in the oven for approximately 35 to 40 minutes or until a thermometer placed in the center of a loin reads 145° F. If the pork is overcooked it will be dry and tough. Slice each tenderloin on the bias across the grain. Makes 20 servings of 3 slices each.

BALSAMIC APPLE SAUCE

½ cup clarified butter
5 Fuji apples, peeled and sectioned into 8 wedges
¾ cup sugar
1½ cups balsamic vinegar
1½ cups heavy cream
1 cup sugar
Cornstarch (if desired to thicken)

When you are ready to make the sauce, heat a large sauté pan over high heat until a drop of water sizzles on the pan. Carefully pour the clarified butter into the hot pan. Place the apple wedges into the hot butter, being careful not to splatter the butter. Sauté the apples until they begin to brown, turning often so they do not burn. Sprinkle the ¾ cup sugar over the cooking apples and continue to cook until the sugar melts and begins to caramelize. Remove pan from heat. Using a pair of tongs, remove apples from pan and place on a platter until ready to serve.

Put the sauté pan with the apple juices and caramelized sugar back onto the stove and heat. Add the balsamic vinegar, stirring to dissolve the caramelized sugar. When the vinegar begins to boil, reduce heat and stir in the heavy cream. Taste the sauce, checking for sweetness. Some balsamic vinegars are more tart than others and you will have to judge how much more sugar to add to the sauce for your own taste. If more sugar is needed, add it in small amounts until the flavor is to your liking. Cook the sauce 2 to 3 minutes until it begins to thicken. Hold the sauce covered over a pan of simmering water until ready to serve. Makes 20 two-ounce portions.

Apricot Cranberry Chicken Breast

GRILLED CHICKEN

20 boneless, skinless chicken breasts
Salt and pepper to taste

Heat a barbecue grill or other grilling surface. Season each chicken breast with salt and pepper. Place on the grill at a 45 degree angle to the grill rack. Grill each breast for approximately 1 minute to mark it. After 1 minute, turn the breast 90 degrees to make a cross-hatch grill mark. After another minute remove each breast and place on an oven-proof cooking tray. The breasts may be stored in a refrigerator for up to 4 hours until ready for service. Approximately 30 minutes before serving time, heat the oven to 350° F. Cook the chicken breasts for 12 to 14 minutes, or until a thermometer placed in the center of the breast reads 165° F. Makes 20 servings.

CRANBERRY APRICOT SAUCE

4 cups canned apricot halves
1 cup fresh or frozen cranberries
¾ cup sugar
¼ teaspoon nutmeg
Cornstarch

Put all ingredients in a saucepan and cook over medium heat until the cranberries have broken. Using a hand mixer, puree the cooked sauce until it is smooth. Thicken slightly with cornstarch slurry (cornstarch and water). Hold in a pan over simmering water at 140° F. until service. Makes 20 servings.

Ham with Pineapple Sauce

7½ pounds ham, sliced into 20 slices
3 cups pineapple juice
1½ cups brown sugar
1 cup water
2 to 3 tablespoons cornstarch

Preheat oven to 350° F. Place ham slices in baking dish. Bake for 12 minutes. Reduce heat to oven's lowest temperature and cover baking dish with foil to keep ham moist. Meanwhile, bring pineapple juice and brown sugar to a boil. Dissolve cornstarch in water then add to boiling juice mixture, stirring until thickened.

When ready to serve, top each warm ham slice with 2 tablespoons of pineapple sauce. Makes 20 servings.

Swiss Chicken

20 boneless, skinless chicken breasts
2 14½-ounce cans chicken broth
10 slices Swiss cheese
3 10¾-ounce cans cream of chicken soup
3½ cups dry stuffing mix

Preheat oven to 350° F. Place chicken breasts on a large baking sheet with 2-inch sides. Pour broth over chicken. Bake at 350° F. for 25 minutes. Pour chicken broth into bowl and save for later. Cover each chicken breast with ½ slice of Swiss cheese. In a medium bowl, blend cream of chicken soup with saved chicken broth. Mix well with whisk. Pour soup mixture over chicken and cheese. Sprinkle 1 tablespoon of dry stuffing mix over each chicken breast. Cover pan with plastic food wrap, then foil. Make sure the foil covers all of the plastic. Bake in oven 1 hour at 225° F. Makes 20 servings.

What bride wouldn't want to serve this delicious meal of chicken with cranberry apricot sauce, confetti risotto, julienned vegetables, and tangy snowpea cucumber salad.

Beef Roulade

2 5-pound eye of round roasts

2 zucchinis

2 onions

2 yellow squash

2 red bell peppers

2 green bell peppers

2 carrots

Salt and pepper to taste

4 feet butcher's twine

¼ cup vegetable oil

Begin preparation by slicing all vegetables lengthwise into ¼-inch strips (about the size and shape of a French fry). Hold vegetables in the refrigerator.

To prepare the beef, first trim the fat from the roasts. Make a ¼-inch deep cut down the length of each roast, running with the grain. Turn each roast so that the cut is ¼ inch above the cutting surface and begin to peel away the outside layer while rolling the beef away from the cut. Continue cutting and unrolling until you are left with a large sheet. Place a layer of plastic wrap over the meat and use a mallet to tenderize and flatten the sheet. Tenderizing will help to expand the sheet and smooth out any uneven spots left from cutting. Season the beef with salt and pepper.

Arrange half of the sliced vegetables on each sheet of beef so that they lay with the grain. You may arrange them in a pattern of colors until the entire beef is covered. Beginning at an edge, roll the beef so that the vegetables lay lengthwise in each roll. Placing the seam down, begin tying the beef with butcher's twine. To tie, gently slide the string under each roll. Wrap the string around each roll and tie it tightly. Place one tie every inch-and-a-half to two inches.

Heat ¼ cup of oil in a large skillet or roast pan. Brown the rolls on all sides. Place the rolls in a 300° F. oven until the rolls reach an internal temperature of 145° F. Remove from the pan and allow rolls to rest for 10 to 15 minutes.

Deglaze the cooking pan to make a pan sauce. Bring the drippings to a boil and thicken with a cornstarch and water slurry. Adjust the sauce's flavor with salt and pepper. Slice the roulade across the grain to reveal the colorful spiral of vegetables. Top with the pan sauce and serve immediately. Makes 24 eight-ounce servings.

Au Gratin Potatoes

16 medium-sized potatoes, cooked
8 tablespoons butter or margarine
8 tablespoons flour
1 tablespoon salt
½ teaspoon pepper
4 cups milk, heated
2 cups cheddar cheese, shredded

Dice cooked potatoes. Melt the butter in a saucepan and stir in the flour and seasonings. Cook, stirring constantly, until the mixture bubbles. Gradually add the milk, and cook over low heat, stirring constantly, until the sauce boils and thickens. Stir in ¾ cup grated cheese and the diced potatoes. Turn into a baking dish, top with the rest of the cheese, and bake at 375° F. about 15 minutes, until the cheese melts and browns. Makes about 20 servings.

Baby Red Potatoes

40 baby red potatoes, 2 per person
1 bunch fresh parsley
4 cloves garlic
½ cup butter
Salt and pepper to taste

Preheat oven to 350° F. Rinse parsley clean and hold on a towel to dry. Pick the parsley leaves from the stems and chop finely. Peel and mince garlic cloves. After washing the potatoes, peel a band of skin away from each, leaving the ends red. Place the potatoes in a saucepan and cover with cool water. Bring the potatoes to a boil; boil until softened. Drain all water. While the potatoes are hot, melt butter and pour over the top. Add minced garlic and sprinkle with parsley. Season with salt and pepper. Place in a roasting pan and bake 15 minutes, or until lightly browned. You may also bake them together with a beef, chicken, or turkey roast, allowing them to absorb roast drippings. Garnish with fresh parsley and serve. Makes 20 servings.

Mashed Potatoes

18 medium potatoes
2 teaspoons salt
½ cup butter
½ cup half-and-half

Peel and quarter potatoes. Cover with cold water. Sprinkle with salt. Bring to a rapid boil; cook over medium heat until tender. Drain water and add butter and half-and-half; beat with a handheld potato masher until light and fluffy. Place in serving bowl and top with an additional square of butter. Serve hot. Makes 20 servings.

Confetti Risotto

3 cups risotto, boiled
1 red pepper, diced
1 green pepper, diced
1 yellow pepper, diced
1 red onion, peeled and diced
¼ cup olive oil
Salt and pepper to taste

Boil the pasta according to directions on package. Clean and dice all the peppers and onion. Heat a sauté pan to sizzling. Add the oil and the peppers and onion. Sauté for 2 minutes only. Mix the risotto with the vegetables just before serving. Add salt and pepper to taste. Makes 20 servings.

OPPOSITE: Beef roulade has great presentation and makes a delicious formal meal or buffet entrée. Served with julienned vegetables and roasted potatoes, it gives your wedding dinner an air of class.

Rice Pilaf

¼ cup butter

3 cups uncooked rice

1 cup onion, diced

1½ cups celery, diced

9 cups hot chicken broth

¼ cup parsley, chopped

¾ cup slivered almonds

Melt butter in hot sauté pan. Add rice, onion, and celery; stir and cook until slightly brown. Add chicken broth. Cover and simmer on low heat until moisture has been absorbed and rice is tender. Add parsley and almonds just before serving. Makes 20 half-cup servings.

Vegetable Medley

8 medium carrots

10 small zucchini

10 ribs celery

¼ cup butter

Salt and pepper to taste

Peel carrots; clean zucchini and celery. Slice vegetables into ½-inch slices on the diagonal. Bring ¼ inch water to a boil and add butter. Add the carrots and simmer, covered, for 4 minutes. Add the celery and simmer an additional 2 minutes. Add the zucchini and continue cooking for an additional 5 minutes, or until vegetables are tender-crisp. Season to taste with salt and pepper. Serve at once, retaining the remaining liquid in the serving dish. Makes 20 servings.

Fresh String Green Beans

5 pounds fresh green beans*

¼ cup butter

¼ teaspoon onion powder

1 clove garlic, peeled and crushed

Seasoned salt to taste

Break ends from beans. Beans should snap when broken; break in thirds. Place in vegetable steamer over boiling water, or cook in a pot of boiling water,

TOP: Swiss chicken is served with fresh asparagus, the perfect vegetable for almost any menu. It is complemented by pink angel dessert, which can also be served as part of a dessert buffet. BOTTOM: This bacon and tomato sandwich is served with an elegant grapefruit and avocado salad.

until tender, about 5 to 6 minutes. Drain and place in serving dish. Melt butter; stir in onion powder and crushed garlic. Toss seasoned butter with green beans. Season to taste with your favorite seasoned salt. Serve immediately. Makes 20 servings.

* Frozen green beans are an option. Follow package instructions to cook beans. Then drain beans and continue following recipe.

Roasted Julienne Root Vegetables

6 large parsnips

6 rutabagas

6 carrots

6 turnips

1 red onion

1 green bell pepper

1 red bell pepper

¼ cup, plus 2 tablespoons olive oil

1 teaspoon salt

½ teaspoon white pepper

3 tablespoons fresh parsley, chopped

Preheat oven to 375° F. Wash all vegetables thoroughly. Peel the parsnips, rutabagas, carrots, turnips, and onion. Halve the bell peppers and discard the seeds. Cut the vegetables into ¼-inch sticks. Place the parsnips, rutabagas, carrots, turnips, red onion, and ¼ cup of the olive oil in a large mixing bowl, season with the salt and pepper and mix to distribute the oil. Spread these vegetables on a large baking pan and place in the oven. For best cooking results avoid stacking more than 2 layers high. Place baking sheet in the oven. In the same bowl mix the bell peppers and remaining olive oil. With a metal spatula turn vegetables every 20 minutes. After 30 minutes add the bell peppers. (Peppers require a shorter cooking time.) Continue turning and cooking until vegetables are lightly browned, about 1 hour, soft but not mushy. Check seasoning; add more salt and pepper if desired. Sprinkle with chopped parsley and serve. Makes 20 servings.

Grapefruit and Avocado Salad

SALAD

5 large oranges

3 fresh grapefruit

5 ripe avocados

3 11½-ounce cans mandarin oranges

2 heads butter lettuce

DRESSING

1½ cups vinegar

1½ cups oil

1½ cups sugar

1½ cups ketchup

2 teaspoons salt

1½ teaspoons garlic powder

1 tablespoon fresh white onion, chopped fine

Combine all ingredients for dressing in a jar and shake well. Chill one hour. Shake again just before serving.

To prepare salad, peel and section oranges and grapefruit. Peel, pit, and slice avocados. Open cans of mandarin oranges and drain. Arrange butter lettuce leaves on plates. Arrange avocado and fruit on top of lettuce. Drizzle dressing over salad just before serving. Makes 20 servings.

Snowpea Cucumber Salad

16 cucumbers

¼ cup sesame seeds

2 cups snowpeas, stemmed

1 recipe Ginger Dressing

Halve the cucumbers and remove the seeds with a spoon. Slice into ½-inch slices diagonally. Put the cucumber slices, sesame seeds, and snowpeas into a bowl. Mix in the Ginger Dressing (see page 76) and serve immediately. Makes 20 servings.

Ginger Dressing

⅓ cup ginger, powdered
2 tablespoons garlic powder
¼ cup sugar
2 cups salad oil
½ cup rice wine vinegar
1 cup honey
2 tablespoons sesame oil
Salt to taste

Mix dry ingredients together. Pour in half of the salad oil, mix thoroughly. Add vinegar and mix well. Slowly add half of the remaining salad oil, whisking the whole time. Add honey and mix well. Slowly add the remaining salad oil and the sesame oil. Adjust flavor with salt.

Lion House Rolls

2 tablespoons yeast
2 cups warm water
⅓ cup sugar
⅓ cup shortening, margarine, or butter
2 teaspoons salt
⅔ cup nonfat dry milk
1 egg
5½ cups all-purpose flour
Butter or margarine, melted

In a large bowl, mix yeast and water and let stand 5 minutes. Add sugar, shortening, salt, dry milk, egg, and 2 cups of the flour. Beat together until smooth. Gradually add remaining flour until soft dough is formed.

Turn onto a lightly floured surface and knead until smooth and elastic. Place in a greased bowl; cover and let rise until dough doubles in bulk. Punch down; divide into thirds.

Roll out one-third of dough into a circle; cut into 12 pie-shaped pieces. Starting at the wide end, roll up each piece into a crescent. Place on greased baking sheet with point on bottom. Repeat with remainder of dough.

Brush tops with melted butter. Let rise until double in size. Bake at 400 F. for 15 minutes. Serve warm. Makes 3 dozen rolls.

Chocolate Silk Pie

2 baked 9-inch pie shells
4 cups milk
2 cups half-and-half
2 tablespoons butter
¾ cup sugar
3 egg yolks
½ cup sugar
¼ teaspoon salt
½ cup cornstarch
⅔ cup plus a few semisweet chocolate chips
1½ teaspoons vanilla
Whipped cream

Reserve up to 1 cup of milk to mix with cornstarch. Place remaining milk in top of a double boiler and add half-and-half, butter, and ¾ cup sugar. Cook until butter is melted and milk looks scalded.

In a bowl, whisk egg yolks until well broken up; then add ½ cup sugar and the salt and whisk together very well. Slowly add this mixture to the hot milk mixture, stirring constantly. Stir for approximately 30 seconds and then allow to cook for 15 to 20 minutes. (This gives the egg time to cook and start the thickening process. Undercooking at this point slows the finished process down by as much as half an hour.)

Mix reserved milk and cornstarch together and slowly add to the hot mixture. Be careful to stir constantly or lumps will form. Continue to stir for at least 2 minutes and every 5 minutes for the next 15 to 20 minutes.

When the pudding is thick, stir in chocolate chips. Stir well until chips are melted. Stir in vanilla. Remove the whole double boiler from stove (the hot water will help keep the pudding hot while you dish up the pies).

Pour filling into pie shells. Fill pies so the tops are a little rounded. Refrigerate 2 hours. When cool, top with whipped cream and garnish with chocolate chips, if desired. Makes 2 pies.

Pink Angel Dessert

½ large angel food or chiffon cake, torn in medium pieces.
1 3-ounce package strawberry gelatin
1¼ cups boiling water
1 8-ounce package frozen, sliced, sweetened strawberries
1 tablespoon sugar
1 dash salt
1 cup whipped cream, whipped with 1 tablespoon sugar
    (or 1 12-ounce carton frozen whipped topping)

In a 9x13-inch pan place half of the cake pieces. Dissolve gelatin in 1¼ cups boiling water. Stir in strawberries, sugar, and salt. Cool until gelatin becomes thick and syrupy. Fold in whipped cream. Pour half of this mixture over the cake pieces in the pan. Place the remainder of the cake in the pan and pour the rest of the strawberry mixture over it. Refrigerate for 1 hour or until it is set. Makes 15 servings.

Lemon Cheesecake

1½ cups graham cracker crumbs, rolled fine
3 tablespoons butter or margarine, melted
3 8-ounce packages cream cheese, softened
1 cup sugar
3 eggs
¾ teaspoon vanilla
⅓ cup lemon juice
1 pint sour cream
3 tablespoons sugar
½ teaspoon vanilla
1½ teaspoons lemon zest
Lemon slices, for garnish

Preheat oven to 325° F. Mix together graham cracker crumbs and butter or margarine. Press firmly into bottom and sides of a 9- or 10-inch springform pan.

In a large mixer bowl whip cream cheese; gradually add sugar. Add eggs one at a time. Stir in vanilla, then stir in lemon juice. Pour filling into crust. Bake 60 minutes. Whip sour cream; add sugar, vanilla, and lemon zest. Spread on top of cheesecake and return to oven. Bake for 10 more minutes. Cool before removing sides from springform pan. Garnish with lemon slices. Refrigerate until ready to serve. Makes 10 to 12 servings.

TOP: This beautiful lemon coconut torte is a light and refreshing dessert. It could be served by the slice on refreshment plates with sliced fruit or as part of a cake buffet. BOTTOM: Lemon cheesecake and an icy drink make lovely choices for service at a summer wedding luncheon.

Formal Wedding Dinners

Formal wedding dinners are usually for the wedding party itself or a smaller group of family and close friends. Because the gathering is for a limited number of people, the meal is often more elaborate. A formal wedding dinner often takes place the night before the wedding and is in place of a wedding breakfast the following day or even in place of the wedding reception itself. You would not offer both a formal wedding dinner and a wedding breakfast to your guests.

Suggested Menus for Formal Wedding Dinners

- Grilled Salmon with Pineapple Raspberry Salsa, Angel Hair Pasta, Asparagus

- Beef Tenderloin with Crab Claws, Roasted Potatoes

- Stuffed Pork Chops, Mashed Potatoes and Gravy, Vegetable Medley, Key Lime Pie

- New York Steak, Brussel Sprouts, Roasted Potatoes, Corn Chowder, Mixed Green Salad

- Chicken Wellington, Rice Pilaf, Fresh String Green Beans, Apple Pomegranate Salad

- Beef Tips in Hunter Sauce, Roasted Potatoes, Sautéed Summer Squash Medley, Lion House Rolls, Chocolate Cream Cake

Grilled Salmon with Pineapple Raspberry Salsa

SALMON

20 salmon filets
Salt and pepper to taste

Heat an outdoor grill until hot. Sprinkle salmon filets with salt and pepper. Grill each filet only long enough to sear grill marks onto the salmon. Turn the salmon 90 degrees to make a square grid on each filet.

Once seared, place the filets on a flat baking tray and store in refrigerator until 30 minutes before serving. At that time, preheat oven to 350° F. and bake filets for approximately 8 minutes. Makes 20 servings.

SALSA

3 cups pineapple, peeled and diced
1 cup red onion, peeled and diced
¾ cup red bell pepper, cored, seeded and diced
¾ cup yellow bell pepper, cored, seeded and diced
1½ tablespoons cilantro, chopped
5 tablespoons lime juice
1 tablespoon jalapeño chili pepper, seeded and chopped
3 tablespoons raspberry vinegar
3 tablespoons olive oil
Salt to taste

Combine all ingredients and season to taste. Cover and refrigerate for at least 1 hour. Serve atop grilled salmon. Makes 24 two-ounce servings.

Beef Tips in Hunter Sauce

7½ pounds beef tenderloin tips, trimmed and cut into thin slices
¼ cup vegetable oil
¼ cup clarified butter
1 medium onion, julienned
2 cloves garlic, chopped
2 cups shiitake mushrooms, stems removed, sliced

2 cups button mushrooms, sliced

½ cup red cooking wine

3 cups brown sauce, available in grocery store

Salt and white pepper to taste

Heat the oil in a sauté pan over high heat. Sauté the beef quickly, until browned on the outside. The beef should be pink inside. Remove the meat from the pan and discard the excess fat. Heat the clarified butter in the sauté pan. Cook the onion, garlic, and the mushrooms until lightly browned. Deglaze the pan with the cooking wine and reduce the juices by about half. Add the brown sauce and reduce the mixture by half. Add the beef and bring the sauce to a boil. Serve immediately. Makes 20 six-ounce servings.

New York Steak

20 6-ounce New York steaks, cut by butcher

4 teaspoons salt

2 teaspoons white pepper

1 teaspoon garlic powder

Heat an electric or gas grill. Mix the salt, pepper, and garlic powder in a small bowl. Place the steaks on a large aluminum sheet tray. Sprinkle each steak with the salt mixture. Grill each steak only long enough to sear grill marks onto each of the steaks. When the marks are seared on, turn the steaks 90 degrees to make a square grid on each steak. Do not cook the steaks long enough to completely cook them. Once marked, place each steak back on the tray. The steaks may be stored in the refrigerator for up to 4 hours before service. Approximately 45 minutes before service, heat an oven to 350° F. Bake the steaks approximately 8 to 10 minutes, depending on how well done you prefer them. Makes 20 servings.

TOP: Salmon with pineapple raspberry salsa is served on a bed of angel hair pasta. BOTTOM: New York steak and corn chowder make a hearty fall or winter menu. They are served here with brussels sprouts and a salad of mixed greens.

Chicken Wellington

20 6-ounce butterfly chicken breasts
1 recipe Stuffing
10 sheets frozen puff pastry dough, thawed
1 egg yolk, beaten
1 recipe Mushroom Sauce

Lay one chicken breast on a clean surface. Place 2 tablespoons stuffing in the center of the breast. Roll the breast around the filling. Cut a sheet of thawed pastry dough in half. Place the rolled breast atop one half of the sheet and fold dough over the top of the breast, sealing the edges with a small amount of water. Cut excess dough from around the chicken, forming a crescent. Pinch dough around the edges to seal. Brush with egg yolk. Repeat with remaining chicken breasts. Bake in a 300° F. oven for 30 minutes. Serve immediately with Mushroom Sauce. Makes 20 servings.

STUFFING

4 tablespoons clarified butter
1 medium onion, peeled and diced
4 cloves garlic, crushed
2 cups ham, diced
3 cups mushrooms, diced
2 teaspoons salt
1 teaspoon pepper

Heat a braising pan and add all ingredients. Sauté until onions are tender. Remove from heat and drain excess liquid from pan.

MUSHROOM SAUCE

½ cup button mushrooms, sliced
1 medium yellow onion, peeled and diced
¼ cup clarified butter
¼ cup flour
2 cups water
3 cups heavy cream
½ cup chicken stock
Egg color, as needed

Sauté mushrooms and onions in clarified butter. Add flour and sauté for 2 minutes. Do not burn flour.

Slowly add water, mixing into a paste. When all the water is added and mixed well, add the cream and chicken base. Slowly bring to a boil, stirring constantly. Be careful not to burn. Add 3 drops egg color to make a light yellow sauce. Strain to smooth sauce. Makes 24 two-ounce servings.

Beef Tenderloin

20 5-ounce filet mignon steaks, cut by butcher
4 teaspoons salt
2 teaspoons white pepper
1 teaspoon garlic powder

Heat an electric or gas grill. Mix the salt, pepper, and garlic powder in a small bowl.

Place the steaks on a large aluminum sheet tray. Sprinkle each steak with the salt mixture. Grill each steak only long enough to sear grill marks onto the meat. When the marks are seared on, turn the steaks 90 degrees to make a square grid on each steak. Do not grill the steaks long enough to completely cook them.

Once marked, place each steak back on the tray. The steaks may be stored in the refrigerator for up to 4 hours before service.

Approximately 45 minutes before service heat an oven to 350° F. Bake the steaks approximately 8 to 10 minutes, depending on how well done you prefer them. Makes 20 servings.

Crab Claws

40 crab claws, purchased frozen
Water
1 tablespoon salt

Fill a medium saucepan with water and 1 tablespoon of salt; bring to a boil. Add the frozen crab claws and simmer for 2 minutes. Remove from the water and serve immediately. Makes 40 servings.

Beef tenderloin served with crab claws over
a toasted crouton topped with choron
sauce is a favorite formal dinner at the
Joseph Smith Memorial Building.

Stuffed pork chops, mashed potatoes, and steamed vegetables make a nice meal for a traditional wedding luncheon. Key lime pie is an unusual twist for dessert.

Stuffed Pork Chops

20 pork chops, 1-inch thick
4 10.5-ounce cans cream of celery soup
¼ cup water

STUFFING

1 cup onion, finely chopped
½ cup celery, finely chopped
¼ cup butter
1 cup chicken stock
1 teaspoon salt
1 teaspoon poultry seasoning
2 teaspoons fresh sage
8 cups ground dry bread crumbs

COATING

2 cups finely ground bread crumbs
1 teaspoon salt
½ teaspoon pepper
2 tablespoons paprika

Have butcher cut a pocket-slit in each pork chop. In a medium skillet, sauté onion and celery in butter. Mix in stock and seasonings. Remove from heat and mix in 8 cups bread crumbs until moistened. Stuff each pork chop with ½ cup stuffing. In a medium bowl, combine 2 cups finely ground bread crumbs, 1 teaspoon salt, ½ teaspoon pepper, and 2 tablespoons paprika. Coat each chop with breading mixture. Place chops in shallow baking dish. Combine celery soup and water and pour over chops. Cover pan tightly with plastic wrap and then with foil. Bake 1½ to 2 hours in a 350° F. oven.

One half hour before serving, pour off gravy and hold chops, covered, in a 225° F. oven. Put gravy in a saucepan (this will be thin), bring to a boil, and thicken with a small amount of cornstarch and water to desired thickness. Serve with mashed potatoes and gravy. Makes 20 servings.

Roasted Potatoes

30 medium new potatoes, quartered
½ cup clarified butter, melted
2 tablespoons fresh parsley, chopped
2 tablespoons fresh thyme, chopped
Salt and pepper to taste

Preheat oven to 350° F. In a large bowl mix clarified butter, parsley, thyme, and salt and pepper. Toss in the quartered potatoes until they are well coated. Spray a jelly-roll pan with nonstick cooking spray. Spread the potatoes evenly on the prepared pan.

Bake in preheated oven for 30 minutes or until the potatoes are tender. Reduce heat in the oven to 170° F. or the lowest temperature your oven will go. Hold until ready to serve. Makes 20 servings.

Sautéed Summer Squash Medley

1 large onion
8 small yellow summer squash
8 small zucchini
2 green peppers
2 red peppers
2 yellow or orange peppers
¼ cup olive oil
2 teaspoons fresh oregano
1 teaspoon fresh basil
2 teaspoons salt
1 cup pitted black olives, sliced
1 cup ricotta cheese, crumbled or 1 cup crumbled mildly
  herbed goat cheese
1 tablespoon fresh squeezed lemon juice

Clean and slice vegetables. Heat oil in a sauté pan; sauté onion until transparent. Add squash, zucchini, and peppers; stir fry over medium heat for 4 minutes or until tender-crisp. Add oregano, basil, and salt. Toss with olives, cheese, and lemon juice. Makes 20 servings.

Apple Pomegranate Salad

14 red delicious apples, cubed
Juice of 2 lemons
2 stalks celery, diced
4 large pomegranates, seeded
3 cups cranberry sauce
1 cup grenadine
Fresh kiwis
Fresh cranberries

Core the apples and set in water that has the juice of 1 lemon added. Dice apples into ½-inch cubes. Dice celery into ½-inch pieces. Remove peeling and all white from pomegranate seeds. Mix apples, celery, pomegranate seeds, cranberry sauce, and grenadine and refrigerate for 1 hour before serving. Garnish with kiwi slices and cranberries. Makes 20 servings.

Corn Chowder

¼ cup butter
1 medium yellow onion, finely diced
1 celery rib, finely diced
2 leeks, finely diced
¼ cup flour
2 quarts chicken stock
1½ cups potatoes, diced into ¼-inch cubes
2 cups whole kernel corn, frozen
8 slices bacon, cooked and finely diced
2 red peppers, finely diced
2 cups heavy cream
2 egg yolks
Salt and pepper to taste

Heat a large stockpot over high heat; add butter, onions, celery, and leeks. Cook until the onion is translucent. Stir in flour until well incorporated. Cook and stir 1 minute. Blend in chicken stock. Add potatoes and reduce heat to medium. Cook, stirring occasionally, for 10 minutes, or until potatoes are tender. Add corn, bacon pieces, and red pepper. Simmer an additional 3 to 5 minutes. Remove pan from heat. In a small bowl, combine cream and egg yolks. Whisk into

chowder. Season with salt and pepper to taste. Serve immediately or refrigerate and reheat for later service. Makes 20 servings.

Key Lime Pie

1½ cups graham cracker crumbs
6 tablespoons butter or margarine, melted
1½ cups sugar
7 tablespoons cornstarch
3 egg yolks
2 cups water
½ cup lime juice
2 tablespoons butter, cut into pieces
1 drop green food coloring

In a 9-inch pie pan, mix graham cracker crumbs with melted butter. Use a fork and level well, then press firmly into bottom and sides of pan. Set aside.

Mix together sugar and cornstarch and place in top of a double boiler not yet on the pan of water.

Place egg yolks in a bowl and whisk until well mixed. Slowly pour half of the water into egg yolks while whisking together. Pour in remaining water. Add egg mixture to sugar mixture in saucepan. Add lime juice and mix well.

Place on top of double boiler. Turn heat on high and cook, stirring every 6 to 7 minutes for 30 to 40 minutes until mixture is clear and thick. (It is important to stir often or the cornstarch will make large lumps.) Cut butter into pieces and add to filling. Add food coloring and stir until well blended. Pour into graham cracker crust. Chill. Makes 8 servings.

Chocolate Cream Cake

1 package devil's food cake mix
Chopped walnuts, if desired

CHOCOLATE FROSTING

4 tablespoons cocoa
3 cups powdered sugar
4 tablespoons butter or margarine, softened
2 to 3 tablespoons evaporated milk
1 teaspoon vanilla

STABILIZED WHIPPING CREAM

1 tablespoon unflavored gelatin

¼ cup cold water

3 cups heavy whipping cream

¾ cup powdered sugar

1½ teaspoons vanilla

Prepare and bake cake mix according to package directions, baking in two 9-inch round layers. Cool and then split both layers horizontally. You will only use three of the four rounds of cake (freeze the extra layer for the next time you make the cake). While cake is baking, prepare Chocolate Frosting and Stabilized Whipping Cream.

To prepare Chocolate Frosting: Mix cocoa and powdered sugar in mixing bowl. Add softened butter, evaporated milk, and vanilla. Beat until smooth.

To prepare Stabilized Whipping Cream: Combine gelatin with water in a small saucepan. Let stand until thick. Over low heat, stir constantly until just dissolved. Remove from heat and allow to cool slightly. (It should still be liquid.) Whip the cream, sugar, and vanilla until slightly thick in a large mixing bowl. Turn mixer on low and gradually add the gelatin, then beat on high until the cream is thick.

Stabilized Whipping Cream will hold up for 4 to 5 days without separating. It can also be used to garnish cheesecakes or in any recipe that calls for whipped cream or nondairy whipped topping.

To assemble the cake: Place one layer of cake on a serving plate. Put half of the Stabilized Whipping Cream on top of the layer of cake. Spread evenly, being careful to leave about a ½-inch border around the edge of the cake with no cream. Then put another layer of cake on top of the cream. Repeat the above steps for a total of five layers—chocolate cake layer, cream layer, chocolate cake layer, cream layer, and chocolate cake layer. Gently push down on the cake to set the layers together. Frost entire cake with Chocolate Frosting. Garnish by sprinkling a few chopped walnuts on the top, if desired.

Buffets

Buffets are a visual feast and a favorite choice for weddings, whether it is a grand dinner buffet for a reception or a lighter buffet for an open house or luncheon. You can create a buffet made entirely of appetizers; a dessert buffet comprised of a variety of favorite desserts; or a cake buffet, offering a wide selection of cakes. A grand buffet is a full dinner buffet. To create a grand buffet, select items from the appetizer and dessert menus, as well as main dishes, a potato or rice dish, salads, vegetables, and breads from the recipes in this book.

Suggested Menu for Appetizer Buffet

Pick three to six of the following:

• Wonton Wrapped Shrimp with Sauce Orientale

• Chicken with Satay Sauce

• Fresh Mozzarella and Tomato Salad

• Coconut Shrimp or Shrimp Crostini

• Crab Cakes with Chili Remoulade or Crab Napolean

• Swedish Meatballs

• Open Face Sandwiches

• Fresh Fruit with Dip

• Fresh Vegetables with Dip

Crab Napoleons, wonton wrapped shrimp, and shrimp crostini are excellent seafood appetizers that add class and sophistication to your wedding.

Crab Napoleon

1 16-ounce package wonton wrappers
1 8-ounce package cream cheese
2 tablespoons Old Bay® seafood seasoning
1 pound crabmeat, defrosted if frozen
1 cup alfalfa sprouts

Heat a deep saucepan or fryer with shortening to 350° F. according to manufacturer's directions. Carefully place individual wonton wrappers into the fry oil and fry until golden brown. The wontons will continue to brown when removed from the oil so care must be taken with this step. Drain on paper towels.

In a medium bowl, mix the cream cheese and the Old Bay seasoning with a metal spoon. (For a stronger flavor, add more Old Bay.) Add the crabmeat and incorporate into the cream cheese. Organize a work area with the crab mixture, fried wontons, and the sprouts within easy reach. Take a wonton skin and spread a small amount of the sprouts onto the skin. Spoon a tablespoon of the crab mixture onto the sprouts. Place on a serving platter and serve immediately or hold for up to 2 hours. Makes 20 servings.

Wonton Wrapped Shrimp with Sauce Orientale

30 to 40 raw shrimp, defrosted
1 12-ounce jar hoisin sauce
2 cups honey
Fresh chives, cut into 2-inch pieces
2 16-ounce packages wonton wrappers
Bowl of water for sealing wrapper skins

In a large bowl, mix the hoisin sauce and the honey. Drain the shrimp. Set up a workstation with separate bowls of shrimp, the hoisin mix, the cut chives, and the wrappers.

Dip one shrimp in the hoisin mixture but do not coat completely. Place the shrimp and two pieces of chive in the wrapper. Roll the wrapper around the shrimp and seal with a small amount of water.

Repeat to finish all the shrimp. Place the shrimp on a sheet tray lined with parchment paper. Store in the refrigerator until service.

About 45 minutes before service, heat the fryer to 350° F. Fry the wrapped shrimp in small batches for 3 minutes, or until almost cooked inside. Serve either on trays for buffet or salad plates with Sauce Orientale puddled below the shrimp.

For a plated appetizer, use three shrimp per person. For buffet service, plan on two shrimp per guest. One bag of shrimp typically yields 30 buffet servings.

SAUCE ORIENTALE

½ yellow onion, peeled and diced
½ bunch thyme
½ bay leaf
4 cups heavy cream
2 tablespoons clarified butter
2 tablespoons flour
2½ tablespoons lobster base
1 tablespoons curry powder
1 cup butter
Salt and white pepper to taste

In a 3-gallon saucepan, sauté the onion, thyme, and bay leaf until the onions become translucent. Add the cream and cook over medium heat to just boiling.

Make a roux in a small sauté pan by heating the clarified butter and then adding the flour. Stir to incorporate the flour. Do not overmix. Cook for one minute. Remove from heat.

When the cream mixture begins to boil, add the roux, a little at a time, to thicken the sauce.

Mix in the lobster base and the curry powder and bring to a boil. Remove from heat and strain through a fine sieve.

Cut the butter into small cubes and add it to the sauce. Finish with salt and white pepper to taste.

Hold in water bath until service. Makes 40 servings.

Shrimp Crostini

20 slices dinner roll (4 rolls cut 5-slices thin)
¼ cup butter, melted
20 large shrimp, cooked
1 8-ounce package cream cheese
1 bunch cilantro, chopped
1 tablespoon lime juice
½ teaspoon salt

Slice the dinner rolls about ¼-inch thick. Brush each slice with the melted butter. Place the slices on a cookie sheet and bake in a preheated 350° F. oven for 6 to 8 minutes, or until golden brown. Meanwhile, whip the cream cheese with a mixer on medium speed. Add the cilantro, lime juice, and salt. Mix until the ingredients are incorporated. Carefully remove the tails from the shrimp by pulling gently so as not to tear off the flesh. The crostini may be made immediately or just before service. Spread an ⅛-inch thick layer of the cream cheese mixture over the toasted bread slices. Place a shrimp on each slice of bread and garnish with a sprig of cilantro. Makes 20 servings.

Coconut Shrimp

1 cup flour
1 cup cornstarch
2 tablespoons Old Bay® seafood seasoning
4 eggs
2 cups cream
2 cups coconut shreds, chopped
60 shrimp
4 cups peanut oil
1 recipe Orange Marmalade Sauce

Combine flour, cornstarch, and seafood seasoning in a bowl. Combine eggs and cream in a separate bowl; beat well. Place shredded coconut in an additional bowl. Coat shrimp, one at a time, with flour mixture and dredge in cream mixture, then roll in shredded coconut. Set the finished shrimp in the refrigerator for at least one hour to set. Just before you are ready to serve the shrimp, heat a large skillet with peanut oil. Fry the shrimp for 3 minutes or until golden brown. Check one shrimp to see if it is done inside. It will no longer be opaque. Serve with Orange Marmalade Sauce. Makes 20 servings of 3 shrimp each.

ORANGE MARMALADE SAUCE

2 tablespoons butter
1 medium onion, diced
½ cup sugar
2 cups mandarin oranges
2 tablespoons cornstarch
2 tablespoons water

Heat a medium saucepan until drops of water sizzle on pan. Add butter and onions. Cook onions until they are caramelized. (You want the onions to be browned to release their sweet flavor.) Add the sugar and the oranges. Cook this until the oranges begin to fall apart.

In a small bowl, mix the cornstarch and water to make a paste. Add cornstarch mixture to sauce in small amounts and thicken until sauce just coats the back of a spoon.

You can hold this sauce in a double boiler set on low for 1 hour before service.

Crab Cakes with Chili Remoulade

1½ pounds crabmeat, picked free of shells
1¼ cups dry bread crumbs
⅓ cup mayonnaise
1½ tablespoons Dijon mustard
¾ teaspoon Tabasco® sauce
1¼ teaspoons salt
Pinch fresh ground black pepper
¾ cup flour
2 eggs, beaten

In medium bowl, combine the crab, ¼ cup of the bread crumbs, the mayonnaise, mustard, Tabasco sauce, salt, and pepper. Shape the mixture into sixteen ¾-inch thick cakes, using about a ¼ cup of the mixture for each. Dust the cakes with the flour and pat off the

Coconut shrimp with orange marmalade sauce makes an impressive and tasty appetizer. The task of creating this recipe is not daunting at all when you follow the simple steps outlined in the recipe and shown at left.

excess. Dip each cake into the eggs and then into the remaining bread crumbs.

In a large nonstick frying pan, heat about ½ inch of oil over moderate heat. When the oil is hot, add some of the crab cakes and fry until golden brown and crisp, 2 to 3 minutes. Turn the cakes and fry them until golden brown on the other side, about 2 minutes longer. Drain on paper towels. Repeat until all the crab cakes are fried. Serve with the Chili Remoulade. Makes 20 servings.

CHILI REMOULADE

2 dried or canned chipolte chilies
½ cup boiling water
2 cups mayonnaise
4 teaspoons Dijon mustard
4 teaspoons lime or lemon juice
½ teaspoon salt

If using dried chilies, place in a small bowl, cover with the boiling water, and let soak 20 minutes. Stem and seed the chilies. Scrape the inside of each chili with a small knife to get the pulp. If using canned chilies, simply remove the seeds.

Put the chilies in a small bowl and stir in the mayonnaise, mustard, lime juice, and salt. Store in refrigerator until ready to serve.

Swedish Meatballs

1 cup milk
½ cup soft bread crumbs
2 pounds lean ground beef
2 eggs, slightly beaten
¼ cup onion, grated
3 tablespoons fresh parsley, chopped
1 tablespoon salt
¼ teaspoon allspice
1 cup beef broth or bouillon

Pour milk in large bowl; stir in crumbs and let soak for a few minutes. Add ground beef, eggs, onion,

parsley, salt, and allspice. Mix together and shape into 36 small balls.

Put meatballs into a large frying pan and cook over medium heat until they are browned on all sides. Pour beef broth over meatballs and simmer, covered, for 15 minutes. Makes 12 servings of 3 meatballs each.

Chicken with Satay Sauce

CHICKEN

2½ pounds chicken breast, sliced ½-inch thick
Salt and pepper to taste

Slice the chicken breast into ½-inch strips. Thread 1 strip of chicken meat onto each skewer. Sprinkle with salt and pepper. Bake in a preheated 350° F. oven for 5 minutes or until a thermometer reads 165° F. Serve with Satay Sauce. Makes 20 servings of 2 skewers each.

SATAY SAUCE

1 medium yellow onion, peeled and diced
3 tablespoons garlic, chopped
2 tablespoons butter
1 14-ounce jar creamy peanut butter
1¾ cups rice wine vinegar
1 tablespoon soy sauce
2 cups water
1 cup cream
1 cup sugar
1 to 2 teaspoons red pepper flakes

Sauté onion and garlic in butter until translucent. Add peanut butter and stir until melted, being careful not to burn. Add vinegar and soy sauce and mix well. Stir in water and cream and return to a boil. Add sugar and mix well. Add red pepper flakes. Makes 24 two-ounce servings.

Fresh Mozzarella and Tomato Salad

2 pounds mozzarella balls, fresh
2 pounds roma tomatoes
¼ cup fresh basil
¼ cup olive oil
1 teaspoon crushed red pepper

Cut the mozzarella balls into ¼-inch thick slices. Slice the tomatoes into ¼-inch thick slices. Separate large basil leaves from the stems. Lay 5 leaves on top of one another and carefully cut the leaves into fine strips; repeat with remaining basil. Add the crushed red pepper to the olive oil and set aside to steep. Using a large serving platter, alternate slices of tomato with slices of mozzarella, working in concentric circles. When the platter is full, drizzle the olive oil and red pepper mixture over the tomatoes and the mozzarella. Finally, sprinkle the shredded basil on top as a garnish. Hold for a maximum of 2 hours before service. Makes 20 servings.

Fruit Dip

2 8-ounce tubs soft-style strawberry cream cheese
1 14-ounce jar marshmallow crème
2 tablespoons orange juice
2 tablespoons lemon juice

In a mixer bowl, beat together cream cheese, marshmallow crème, and fruit juices. Beat until smooth. Refrigerate before serving. Serve with fresh fruit. Makes 20 servings.

Open Face Sandwiches

BREADS

A variety of white, wheat, rye, pumpernickel, and sourdough breads

HAM SPREAD

1 8-ounce tub soft-style cream cheese with chives and onion
½ teaspoon Dijon mustard

1 tablespoon mayonnaise
⅓ cup ham, fully cooked and finely chopped

To make ham spread, stir together cream cheese, mustard, mayonnaise, and ham in a small mixing bowl. Cover and chill. Makes 20 servings.

ALMOND-BACON CHEESE SPREAD

¼ cup unblanched almonds, roasted and finely chopped
2 strips bacon, cooked and crumbled
1 cup Velveeta® cheese, grated
1 tablespoon green onion, chopped
½ cup mayonnaise

To make almond-bacon cheese spread, combine almonds, bacon, Velveeta, green onion, and mayonnaise. Mix lightly. Store in refrigerator until ready to serve. Makes 20 servings.

GREEN CHILI ARTICHOKE SPREAD

1 14-ounce can artichoke hearts, drained
1 6-ounce jar marinated artichoke hearts, drained
1 cup cheddar cheese, shredded
1 3-ounce package cream cheese
1 4-ounce can diced green chili peppers, drained

To make green chili artichoke spread, place drained artichoke hearts and marinated artichoke hearts in a blender or food processor. Cover and process until finely chopped, stopping to scrape down sides as necessary. Put blended artichokes in medium saucepan, then stir in cheddar cheese, cream cheese, and chili peppers. Heat over low heat, stirring constantly for 12 to 15 minutes or until the cheese is melted and the mixture is heated through.

Make sandwiches using one or all of the spreads, on one type or a variety of breads. Use bread that is sliced lengthwise, if possible. Coat each slice of bread with the spread of your choice. Cut crusts off bread. (Note: it is much easier to cut crusts off bread after you have covered it with the spread.) For bread that is sliced lengthwise, cut into one-inch slices. Cut regular sandwich bread into triangles by cutting each slice of bread diagonally into quarters.

Serve with garnishes such as a small carrot curl, half a cherry tomato, a thin slice of pickle, a slice of black olive, or a small sprig of parsley, if desired. Store in refrigerator until ready to serve. Makes 20 servings.

TOP LEFT: *Sliced fruit and a refreshing fruit dip are easy to prepare and perfect for an afternoon luncheon or even a bridal shower.* TOP RIGHT: *Don't forget the appeal of fresh vegetables and dip at any gathering. Vegetables are available year round and can be cut and sliced to make a beautiful and colorful presentation at your buffet table.* BOTTOM: *This fresh mozzarella and tomato salad adds color and flavor to any meal. Serve it as a dish in a grand buffet, as an appetizer, or as a salad for a plated meal.*

Refrigerator Rolls

1 cup milk
¼ cup butter or margarine
¼ cup sugar
1 tablespoon yeast
1 tablespoon sugar
¼ cup lukewarm water
2 teaspoons salt
4 cups all-purpose flour
3 eggs
2 tablespoons butter, melted

In a small saucepan, scald the milk. Add butter and ¼ cup sugar to hot milk. Cool. Combine yeast, 1 tablespoon sugar, and lukewarm water. Let stand 5 minutes to soften yeast.

Add salt to flour; set aside. In a large bowl, combine milk and yeast mixtures, and add 1 cup of the flour. Add eggs and beat well. Continue adding flour gradually, beating until smooth after each addition. (This is a soft dough, and most or all of the flour can be handled by an electric mixer.)

Cover bowl and place out of draft. Let dough rise until it doubles in size. Punch down. Cover again and place in refrigerator overnight, or until thoroughly chilled. (Dough will keep well up to 3 days.) When ready to use, remove from refrigerator and roll and shape while cold. (You can handle a much softer dough if it is chilled.) Place on greased pans. Brush dough with melted butter. Let rolls rise 1 to 1½ hours. Bake rolls at 375° F. for 10 to 15 minutes or until done. Makes 2½ dozen rolls.

Waldorf Salad

7 cups Fuji apples, cored and diced
3 cups celery, diced
½ cup walnuts, coarsely chopped
1 cup raisins

DRESSING

3 cups heavy whipping cream
¾ cup sugar
1 teaspoon vanilla extract
¼ cup sour cream

In a large clean bowl whip the cream using an electric mixer. Gradually add the sugar as the cream whips.

Just before the cream reaches the soft peak stage add the vanilla. Continue whipping until the cream is at the soft peak stage.

Add the sour cream and whip until incorporated. Cover and place the bowl in the refrigerator until the remaining ingredients are completed.

Chop the nuts and the celery before cutting the apples. Fuji apples will not brown as fast as other apples but you will have to work quickly when cutting them.

After the apples are cut, toss the apples, walnuts, and celery in a bowl. Mix in the dressing and serve immediately. Makes 20 servings.

Potato Salad

10 large baking potatoes
2 whole eggs, hard boiled
½ bell pepper, diced
5 bacon strips, cooked and crushed
4 cups mayonnaise
2 tablespoons tarragon
1 tablespoon thyme
½ cup sweet relish

1 tablespoon Old Bay® seafood seasoning

½ teaspoon salt

½ tablespoon white pepper

½ cup rice wine vinegar

¼ cup sugar

Peel potatoes and cook in salted water; drain. When cool, chop into a large bowl. Peel and dice hard-boiled eggs; add to potatoes. Add bell pepper and bacon. Mix remaining ingredients in a small bowl until smooth. Pour dressing mixture over potato mixture and stir until well coated. Makes 24 servings.

Suggested Menu for Dessert Buffet

Pick three to six of the following:

- Apricot Meringue Sponge Cake

- Dipped Strawberries

- Fruit Tarts

- Chocolate Walnut Cake

- Eclairs

- Crème Brûlée

- Chocolate Mousse

- Lemon Cheesecake

- Pavlova

Apricot Meringue Sponge Cake

15 eggs

2 cups sugar

2 cups cake flour, sifted

1 12-ounce jar of apricot jelly

MERINGUE TOPPING

6 egg whites

1½ cups sugar

1 tablespoon cornstarch

1 teaspoon vanilla

½ cup pistachio nuts, crushed

Preheat the oven to 350° F. Beat the eggs and sugar in a clean stainless steel mixing bowl until light yellow in color and double in volume. Add the sifted cake flour ½ cup at a time until it is all incorporated.

Spray 2 jelly-roll pans with nonstick pan spray and line with parchment paper. Pour half of the batter into each pan. Bake for 20 to 25 minutes or until a toothpick inserted in the center of the cake comes out clean. Times will vary depending on the oven used.

Remove from oven and cool in the pan.

When the cakes are cooled, remove them from the pan. Spread one layer with apricot jam and sandwich the two layers together.

To make the meringue topping: Add egg whites to a clean, dry stainless steel bowl. Mix sugar and cornstarch together and add these to the egg whites. Add vanilla. Beat until soft peaks form. Spread the meringue on the top layer of the cake. Sprinkle with crushed pistachio nuts. Cut the petit fours into 60 pieces—3 per guest for a party of 20.

Chocolate Walnut Cake

5 eggs

4½ cups sugar

4½ cups sour cream

1 tablespoon baking soda

4 cups sweetened condensed milk

1 tablespoon vanilla extract

1 tablespoon rum extract

6 cups walnuts, chopped fine

½ cup cocoa powder

9 cups cake flour, sifted

Beat the eggs and sugar in a clean stainless steel bowl using an electric mixer on high speed until the eggs turn a lemon yellow color.

Beat in the sour cream, baking soda, condensed milk, vanilla, and rum extract. Continue beating and add the walnuts. Mix for 5 minutes.

Mix the cocoa and flour in a separate bowl. Set the mixer on low speed and slowly add the flour mixture. Do not overbeat.

Apricot meringue sponge cake squares, tuxedo dipped strawberries, mini fruit tarts, chocolate cake triangles, eclairs, crème brûlée, and chocolate mousse.

Spray 3 jelly-roll pans with nonstick pan spray and line with parchment paper. Pour about a third of the batter into each pan. Bake for 20 to 25 minutes or until a toothpick inserted in the center of the cake comes out clean. Times will vary depending on the oven used. Makes 12 to 14 servings.

Eclairs

1 cup cold water
½ cup butter or margarine
1 cup all-purpose flour
¼ teaspoon salt
4 eggs, fresh, at room temperature
1 recipe Vanilla Pudding
1 recipe Chocolate Frosting

Preheat oven to 375° F. In a large saucepan, bring water and butter to a rolling boil. While the water and butter are boiling and still on the stove, add flour and salt. Stir until mixture clings together. Remove from stove and place in a medium mixer. Add one egg at a time, mixing on low speed until each egg is incorporated. The batter should be shiny and smooth. Do not overwhip; too much air causes the shells to be bumpy and misshapen. Force dough through a decorating tube onto paper-lined baking sheets in strips about 3 inches long. Bake at 375° F. for 25 minutes.

When pastry is cool, slice off tops and scoop out any uncooked dough that may be remaining. Fill with Vanilla Pudding. Replace tops. Frost with Chocolate Frosting. Keep refrigerated until ready to serve. Makes approximately 36 eclairs.

Vanilla Pudding

2 cups 2% milk
¼ cup sugar
2 tablespoons cornstarch
¼ teaspoon salt
1 teaspoon vanilla

Heat milk in the top of a double boiler until very hot. Combine sugar, cornstarch, and salt in a small bowl and stir in ½ cup of the hot milk. Stir until sugar is dissolved. Add sugar mixture slowly to the hot milk in double boiler, stirring constantly. Cook and stir until mixture thickens and is smooth, about 3 minutes. Cover and cook 5 minutes longer. Remove from heat and stir in vanilla. Cover with plastic wrap and let stand until cool. Refrigerate for 3 hours before serving. Makes 4 servings of pudding, or fills one batch of eclairs.

Chocolate Frosting

¼ cup cocoa
3 cups powdered sugar
¼ cup butter or margarine, softened
2 or 3 tablespoons milk
1 teaspoon vanilla

Mix cocoa and powdered sugar in mixing bowl. Add butter, milk, and vanilla. Beat until smooth.

Crème Brûlée

6 cups heavy cream
1 cup egg yolks (this is about 12)
¾ cup sugar
1 teaspoon vanilla extract
1½ cups sugar, for glazing

In a heavy copper pot heat cream until just scalded. Mix—do not whip—egg yolks, ¾ cup sugar, and vanilla. Set aside. In a copper pot, melt the 1½ cups sugar, stirring continuously until it takes on a light caramel color. Time caramelized sugar and cream mixture to be ready at the same time. Slowly pour the caramelized sugar into the cream mixture. A hand mixer works well for this. Mix only until blended. Skim off the foam and cool before baking. Pour the brûlée mixture into ramekins about 4 ounces in size. Place the filled ramekins into a water bath about three quarters up the sides of the ramekins. Bake in a 300° F. oven for 50 to 60 minutes. Brûlée is done when the center is set. Cool; sprinkle granulated sugar on each brûlée. Place under a broiler and watch carefully. Remove from heat when sugar bubbles. Serve warm or chilled. Makes 20 servings.

Fruit Tarts

20 prepared tart shells
8 ounces bittersweet chocolate, melted
1 recipe Basic Pastry Cream
Seasonal Fruit

Cook the tartlets according to directions on the box. When the tartlet shells are cooled, brush each with the melted chocolate. Spoon in pastry cream to just below the edge of the shell. Decorate each tartlet with slices of seasonal fruit. Suggested fruits include berries, kiwi slices, peach slices, edible flowers, and mandarin orange slices. Tartlets can be refrigerated up to 6 hours before service. Makes 20 tarts.

BASIC PASTRY CREAM

3¾ cups sugar
¾ cup plus ½ tablespoon cornstarch
⅝ teaspoon salt
10 cups milk
15 egg yolks, beaten
10 tablespoons butter
5 teaspoons vanilla extract

Mix sugar, cornstarch, salt, and milk together in a heavy saucepan until sugar is dissolved. Bring to a boil over medium-high heat, stirring constantly. Cook 2 minutes, until thick and clear. Remove a spoonful of the cream mixture and stir into beaten egg yolks. Add egg mixture to cream and cook until mixture begins to boil again. Stir constantly. Remove from heat. Add butter and vanilla extract, stirring until butter is melted. Cover with plastic wrap. Place wrap so that it touches the pudding. This will prevent a film from forming. Refrigerate. Pastry cream can be thinned by adding lightly whipped cream once the pastry cream has cooled. It can also be flavored with lemon curd. Makes enough cream to fill 20 tartlet shells.

Chocolate Mousse

4 tablespoons unsalted butter
12 ounces dark chocolate, broken up
6 eggs, separated
2 cups heavy cream
½ cup powdered sugar

Melt the butter and chocolate in the top of a double boiler set over simmering water. Stir until smooth. Pour into a large bowl and cool slightly.

Beat the egg yolks until blended and light yellow in color. Incorporate yolks into melted chocolate mixture. In a medium bowl, whip the cream until soft peaks form. Add powdered sugar and beat until stiff but not dry. Fold into the chocolate mixture. In a medium bowl beat the egg whites until stiff but not dry. Fold into the chocolate and cream mixture. Chill for service. Makes 16 servings.

Pavlova

6 egg whites
3 cups sugar
3 teaspoons vanilla
3 teaspoons vinegar or lemon juice
½ cup boiling water
1 cup whipping cream
½ teaspoon vanilla
1 jar apricot preserves
Fresh fruit slices, such as peaches, strawberries, pineapple, blueberries, kiwi

Preheat oven to 450° F. Bring egg whites to room temperature. Line a baking sheet with foil. Using an 8-inch round cake pan as a guide, draw a circle on the foil.

In a large electric mixer bowl, beat together egg whites, sugar, 3 teaspoons vanilla, vinegar or lemon juice, and boiling water. Beat on high speed for about 12 minutes, scraping bowl constantly, until stiff peaks form and mixture holds its shape but is not dry. Spread the mixture onto the circle on the baking tray. Shape

into a pie-shell form with a spoon, making the bottom ½-inch thick and the sides 2½ to 3 inches high. Form the edges into peaks or make a rim around the edge. Place baking sheet in center of preheated oven and turn oven off. Let stand 4 to 5 hours. Do not open oven door.

To serve: Remove meringue shell from foil and place on a serving plate. Whip cream with the ½ teaspoon vanilla until soft peaks form; spread in shell. In a small saucepan, warm the preserves until liquid. Arrange sliced fresh fruit on top of whipped cream and brush with melted preserves. Cut and serve immediately. Makes 20 servings. *Note:* Pavlova can be made into individual portions as pictured above.

Dipped Strawberries

1 pound high-quality milk chocolate
12 to 16 large strawberries, rinsed and thoroughly dried

Melt chocolate in a double boiler over low heat (do not let the water boil). Carefully dip rinsed and dried strawberries into melted chocolate, covering three-fourths of the berry and leaving the stem end

clean. Place each strawberry onto a cookie sheet lined with parchment or waxed paper. Refrigerate until chocolate is set. Makes 12 to 16 dipped strawberries.

TUXEDO STRAWBERRIES

1 pound high-quality milk chocolate
1 pound high-quality white chocolate
12 to 16 large strawberries, rinsed and thoroughly dried.

Follow directions under dipped strawberries for separately melting both milk and white chocolates. After lining a cookie sheet with waxed paper and rinsing and drying strawberries, follow these steps:

1. Dip the front of each strawberry in white chocolate and set aside to harden.

2. Dip the sides of each strawberry in milk chocolate at a 45° angle, making sure to leave enough of the white chocolate in the center to look like a shirt underneath a tuxedo jacket. You may have to dip each berry two or three times to get the right amount of chocolate.

3. Use a toothpick to dab on 3 milk-chocolate buttons. Make a bow tie by placing two large dots side by side and pulling them together in the middle with the end of the toothpick. Allow chocolate to harden before serving.

LEFT: Making chocolate dipped strawberries that look like tuxedos is easier than it looks. Simply follow the step-by-step process for these tiny delights.
RIGHT: Pavlova made of meringue and fresh fruit is an excellent choice for a dessert buffet or served individually as a refreshment plate.

TOP: *A cake buffet can have as few as three different cakes and as many as twelve. Cake buffets are a great way to serve guests at a large wedding reception. Pictured here: Raspberry cheesecake, toffee torte, German chocolate cake, lemon cheesecake, lemon coconut torte, dipped strawberries, sting of the bee cake, carrot cake, double chocolate raspberry cake, chocolate cheesecake, strawberry torte, chocolate cream cake.* BOTTOM LEFT: *Chocolate cakes are perennial favorites. A slice of double chocolate raspberry cake, toffee torte, and chocolate cheesecake are excellent choices whether you offer just one or a choice of all three.* BOTTOM RIGHT: *Lion House cheesecake.*

Lion House Cheesecake

1½ cups graham cracker crumbs
3 tablespoons sugar
6 tablespoons butter or margarine, melted
3 8-ounce packages cream cheese, softened
1 cup sugar
3 eggs
¾ teaspoon vanilla
1 tablespoon lemon juice
1 pint sour cream
3 tablespoons sugar
½ teaspoon vanilla

In a medium bowl thoroughly mix together graham cracker crumbs, 3 tablespoons sugar, and butter. Press firmly into a 10-inch deep dish pie pan or springform pan, lining the bottom and sides. Set aside.

To make filling, place cream cheese in a large mixer bowl and beat well. Add 1 cup sugar a little at a time. Add eggs one at a time. Add ¾ teaspoon vanilla and 1 tablespoon lemon juice. Combine thoroughly. Pour filling into crust; fill to within ½ inch of top to allow room for topping. Bake 55 to 60 minutes at 300° F. While cheesecake is baking, prepare topping.

To make topping, place sour cream in a small mixer

bowl and whip; add 3 tablespoons sugar gradually. Add ½ teaspoon vanilla. Pour filling over top of cheesecake and return to oven; bake for an additional 10 minutes. Allow to cool. Refrigerate until ready to serve. Makes 10 to 12 servings.

Sting of the Bee Cake

BATTER

1 cup butter (no substitutes)
⅔ cup sugar
2 eggs
3 cups sifted flour
3 tablespoons baking powder
1 teaspoon salt
½ cup milk

TOPPING

½ cup butter
1 cup almonds, finely chopped
½ cup sugar
2 tablespoons milk
2 tablespoons vanilla

FILLING

1 cup butter, softened
2 egg yolks
2 cups powdered sugar
2 teaspoons vanilla
½ cup raspberry jam

Preheat oven to 375° F. To make topping, melt butter in a small saucepan; blend in chopped almonds, sugar, milk, and vanilla. Bring to a boil. Remove from heat and allow to cool while making the batter.

To make batter, cream butter; gradually add sugar, creaming well. Beat in eggs, one at a time, until light and fluffy. Add sifted dry ingredients alternately with milk. Spread batter into a well-greased 9-inch springform pan.

Spread topping carefully over batter. Bake cake for 50 minutes. Remove from oven and cool completely. Remove sides from springform pan. Prepare filling.

To make filling, cream butter. Beat in egg yolks, powdered sugar, and vanilla. Split cake horizontally into two layers. Spread bottom layer with filling; spread raspberry jam over top. Very carefully replace top layer of cake. Cut vertically into thin slices and serve. Makes 16 to 20 servings.

Toffee Torte

1 package devil's food cake mix
1 16-ounce carton frozen whipped topping, thawed
7 English toffee bars (such as Heath® or Skor®), crushed

Grease and flour two 9-inch round cake pans. Prepare and bake the cake according to package directions. Cool on a wire rack. (If time permits, the cakes can be frozen for easier handling.) Carefully cut each layer horizontally to make 2 layers. Place whipped topping in a bowl and fold in 6 of the crushed candy bars. Place one layer of the cake on a serving plate and spread with topping mixture. Repeat with remaining three layers. Frost the sides and top with the topping mixture. Sprinkle the remaining crushed candy bar on top of the cake. Makes 12 to 14 servings.

Lemon Coconut Torte

1 white or yellow cake mix
1 12-ounce container frozen whipped topping
2 cups coconut, flaked
2 15½-ounce cans lemon pie filling

Grease and flour two 9-inch round cake pans. Set aside. Prepare and bake cake according to package directions. (Make sure you use the high altitude directions if they apply to your area.) Allow cakes to cool on wire racks.

Slice cakes in half horizontally. Place first layer of cake on a serving plate and spread two-thirds of a can of lemon pie filling on the top of the cake. Place next layer of cake on top of filling. Spread with about a ¼-inch layer of whipped topping and place the next layer of cake on top. Spread ⅔ of a can of lemon pie filling on cake and place the last layer of cake on top. Frost top and sides of entire cake with remaining whipped topping. Cover sides of cake with coconut.

Spread remaining pudding on top of cake and sprinkle with a small amount of coconut. This cake should be refrigerated. Makes 12 to 14 servings.

Carrot Cake

1 cup sugar
½ cup oil
2 eggs, beaten
1½ cups grated carrots
1 cup unsifted flour
½ teaspoon salt
1 teaspoon soda
1 teaspoon cinnamon
¼ cup ground coconut
¼ cup nuts
¼ cup raisins

FROSTING

1 8-ounce package cream cheese, softened
¼ cup margarine, at room temperature
2½ cups powdered sugar
Hot water, as needed

Preheat oven to 400° F. Lightly grease and flour a 9x9-inch square cake pan. Set aside. Combine sugar and oil in a large mixing bowl. Add eggs; mix well. Add grated carrots. Slowly stir in sifted dry ingredients. Add coconut, nuts, and raisins and mix well. Pour batter into prepared pan and bake for 20 to 30 minutes or until cake tests done. When cool, spread with cream cheese frosting. Makes 12 to 14 servings.

To prepare frosting, cream together cream cheese, margarine, and sugar in a mixer bowl. Add a little hot water, one teaspoon at a time, until you reach desired spreading consistency.

Sting of the bee cake is a traditional
favorite at the Lion House.

Refreshment Plates

Refreshment plates are a popular and inexpensive choice for a wedding reception. And the variety of plates you can create is endless. A more elaborate plate might include a soft roll filled with chilled chicken salad, fresh berries garnished with a sprig of mint, and a rich chocolate truffle. A single specialty dessert is also an excellent choice; perhaps a thick slice of New York-style cheesecake covered with fresh berries and set atop a puddle of chocolate sauce.

Refreshment plates are commonly served to guests as they seat themselves at open-seating tables, and cleared away as the guests finish and move on for the evening. Refreshment plates can also be created buffet style; in this case guests serve themselves, but you will still need to have servers on hand to clear the tables.

Suggested Menus for Refreshment Plates

- Hot Creamed Chicken in a Puff Pastry, Melon Slices and a Fresh Strawberry

- Cold Chicken Salad on a Croissant, Melon Balls and Mango Slices

- Roast Turkey Breast Tea Sandwiches with Apricot Cranberry Relish, Fresh Berries

- Ham Sandwiches, Fresh Vegetables and Dip

- Ribbon Sandwiches, Dipped Pretzels, Strawberry Tarts

- Berry Frappe, German Chocolate Cookies, Dipped Strawberries

- Lion House Cheesecake or Eclairs

- Slice of Wedding Cake with Mint and Nut Cup

Cold Chicken Salad on a Croissant

20 croissants
4 pounds boneless, skinless chicken breasts, thawed
2 tablespoons salt
½ cup onion, peeled and diced
½ cup celery, diced
¾ cup walnuts, chopped
1½ cups mayonnaise
Salt and white pepper to taste

Fill a large stockpot with water and 2 tablespoons of salt. Bring to a boil. Place the chicken breasts in the boiling water and cook until the juices run clear or the meat is 165° F. on a thermometer.

Remove the pot from the stove. Remove the chicken from the pot and place in a large glass baking dish, spreading the chicken out to help it cool. Place the chicken breasts in the refrigerator for 4 hours or until the chicken is completely cooled.

In a large bowl combine the onion, celery, walnuts, mayonnaise, and salt and pepper. Mix with a large spoon. Cut the cooled chicken into strips. Mix the cut chicken with the ingredients already in the bowl. Season with additional salt and white pepper to taste. Chicken salad can be made up to one day in advance. Holding the salad any longer will bring out the unpleasant aftertaste of onion. Store in the refrigerator until ready to serve. Serve on a croissant. Makes 20 croissants.

Hot Creamed Chicken in a Puff Pastry

20 puff pastries
2 tablespoons clarified butter
1 cup onion, finely diced
2 cloves garlic, minced
8 cups chicken, diced
1 teaspoon fresh thyme, chopped
4 cups chicken stock
1 pint heavy cream
Salt and pepper to taste

Sauté onion and garlic in clarified butter until

translucent; do not let brown. Add diced chicken and thyme and cook until done. Add chicken stock and cream and bring to a boil; let reduce to a thick consistency. Add salt and pepper to taste. Spoon into puff pastries and serve immediately. Makes 20 servings.

Note: Chicken stock can be replaced by a good quality chicken base. Do not use bouillon cubes—they contain too much salt.

Ribbon Sandwiches

2 loaves of bread, sliced horizontally (this can be ordered
    through most bakeries; ask for ribbon sandwich bread)
I recipe Cream Cheese Filling
Mayonnaise
I recipe Chicken Salad Filling
Paprika
Parsley flakes

CREAM CHEESE FILLING

I 8-ounce package cream cheese, softened
1¼ cups crushed pineapple, drained slightly
¼ cup sugar

Combine all ingredients and mix well.

CHICKEN SALAD FILLING

4 cups cooked chicken, shredded
I cup celery, finely minced
⅓ cup yellow onion, finely minced
½ teaspoon salt
Pepper to taste
I cup mayonnaise

Combine all ingredients and stir until well blended.

Using 3 slices of bread (loaf sliced horizontally), spread cream cheese mixture on bottom layer. Add the next layer of bread, spread with a small amount of mayonnaise, then cover layer with the chicken mixture. Add the last layer of bread, spreading top and bottom with mayonnaise. If desired, sprinkle top with paprika and dry parsley flakes. Trim crusts on all four sides. Slice each loaf into 12 sandwiches. Makes approximately 24 sandwiches.

Roast Turkey Breast Tea Sandwiches with Apricot Cranberry Relish

RELISH

3½ cups fresh cranberries
I cup canned apricot nectar
I cup sugar
2 tablespoons dried cranberries
2 tablespoons dried apricots, thinly sliced
½ teaspoon pure vanilla extract

In a medium stainless steel saucepan, combine the cranberries, apricot nectar, and sugar and bring to a boil over moderately high heat. Reduce the heat to low, add the dried cranberries and apricots, cover and cook, stirring occasionally, until slightly reduced, about 20 minutes.

Drain the cranberries, reserving ¼ cup of the cooking liquid. Stir the vanilla into the reserved liquid. Add the drained fruits and let cool. Makes 20 two-ounce servings.

SANDWICHES

40 slices whole wheat bread, toasted
4 pounds turkey breast, sliced
Salt and freshly ground white pepper to taste
80 scallions, green part only
40 romaine lettuce leaves

Spread 2 slices of the bread with about 1½ tablespoons each of the relish. Layer the turkey on the relish and season with salt and pepper. Top with the scallions, romaine lettuce, and the remaining bread.

The relish can be refrigerated for up to 1 week. The sandwiches can be refrigerated for up to 3 hours. Makes 20 sandwiches.

A favorite choice of many brides is cold chicken salad on a croissant.

Dipped Pretzels

2 12-ounce packages semisweet chocolate chips
2 12-ounce packages white chocolate chips
1 16-ounce bag pretzel knots

Line 2 cookie sheets with parchment or waxed paper. Place semisweet chips in the top of a double boiler and place over simmering water. Stir occasionally until chips are melted. If you want 2-toned decorations, you will need to melt the white chips in a separate pan at the same time. (You can also melt the chips in a glass bowl in the microwave in 30-second increments.) Pick up the pretzel by the single round loop and dip the double loop in the chocolate almost to your fingertips. Lay the pretzel on waxed paper to dry. You may choose to leave parts of the pretzel exposed or dip the other half in white chocolate after the semisweet chocolate has dried. You can also use the chocolate to "bond" several pretzels together in a variety of creative designs.

German Chocolate Cookies

6 tablespoons raisins
1 cup nuts
1 cup sugar
½ cup shortening
2 teaspoons corn syrup
6 tablespoons cocoa
1½ teaspoons salt
3 eggs
½ teaspoon vanilla
1¾ cups all-purpose flour
1 can ready-to-serve coconut pecan frosting
1 recipe Chocolate Ganache

To make cookies: Preheat oven to 350° F. Mix nuts and raisins together and grind in a blender until very fine. Set aside. In a large mixing bowl, cream sugar and shortening until light and fluffy. Add corn syrup, cocoa, salt, eggs, and vanilla; mix well. Add nut and raisin mixture and the flour. Mix well. Drop by rounded teaspoonfuls on a wax paper–lined or well-greased cookie

TOP: A ribbon sandwich, dipped pretzels, and strawberry tart make an appetizing refreshment plate. BOTTOM: A roasted turkey tea sandwich can be part of a fancy refreshment plate or be served as a light lunch.

sheet. Bake for 8 to 10 minutes. While cookies are cooling prepare Ganache.

Turn the chocolate cookies upside down. On the flat side of each cookie place 1 teaspoon coconut pecan frosting. When you have a pan full of cookies frosted, stir the Ganache and, with a fork, drizzle it all over the coconut pecan frosting. (It should look like chocolate strings of different lengths and thickness). Makes 60 cookies.

CHOCOLATE GANACHE

½ cup heavy whipping cream

2 teaspoons butter

1 cup semisweet chocolate chips

Pour cream into a small saucepan and boil for 1 minute, stirring constantly. Remove from heat and add butter and chocolate chips; stir until completely melted and smooth. If mixture gets too thick to use return it to medium heat on stove and reheat, stirring constantly.

Strawberry Tarts

4 to 5 pints fresh strawberries, washed, hulled, and cut in
    quarters or smaller if the berries are large

Whipped cream, if desired

TART SHELLS

¼ cup butter

⅓ cup lard

¼ cup margarine

⅓ cup shortening

1 tablespoon sugar

½ teaspoon baking powder

1 teaspoon salt

1 tablespoon nonfat dry milk (powdered)

1½ cups pastry flour

1½ cups bread flour

½ cup cold water (may need 1 tablespoon more)

STRAWBERRY GLAZE

6 cups water

2 cups sugar

2 3-ounce packages strawberry-flavored gelatin

6 tablespoons cornstarch

TOP: German chocolate cookies, strawberries dipped in white chocolate, and a strawberry frappe make the perfect refreshment plate for a summer wedding. BOTTOM: Hot creamed chicken in a puff pastry is reminiscent of the warmth of a home-cooked meal and is the perfect appetizer for a formal dinner or for service on a refreshment plate with fruit and a sweet treat.

In a mixer, cream together butter, lard, margarine, and shortening. In a bowl, mix the sugar, baking powder, salt, and dry milk powder together. Then add to the creamed butter mixture and mix briefly. Add pastry flour and beat until it is blended. Add bread flour and mix slightly. Pour water in and beat again only until water is incorporated.

Roll dough out on floured board about ¼-inch thick. With a fork prick holes all over the dough. With a 3-inch round cookie cutter cut the dough in circles. Place muffin tins upside down on your counter and place one circle of dough on top of each cup. Allow dough to form around cup. Bake in a 375° F. oven for 8 to 10 minutes. Shells should be light golden brown. (They will continue to cook after they have been removed from the oven so don't let them get too brown.) When the shells are completely cool carefully lift them off the pan and turn right side up so they can be filled.

To prepare glaze, bring water and sugar to a boil in a large saucepan. Mix gelatin with cornstarch; gradually add to boiling mixture. Cook over medium-high heat, stirring constantly for 5 minutes or until mixture is clear and thickened slightly. Let stand at room temperature until just warm, about 30 minutes. Pour over fresh strawberries and gently fold together. Fill tart shells. Serve with whipped cream on top if desired. Makes 15 tarts.

Drinks

Drinks are rarely served as the entire refreshment offering for a wedding, though a fancy fresh fruit frappe might possibly be enough for an outdoor summer wedding reception. Even in that case, it is usually complemented with fresh fruit, an assortment of sugar cookies, or a slice of wedding cake. Drink recipes, however, can complement almost any wedding menu, and by the choice of a drink alone you can do a lot toward setting the style and tone of your wedding.

Suggested Drinks

- Mango Otai
- Watermelon-Coconut Otai
- Apple Otai
- Berry Frappe
- Lime Slush
- Cranberry Punch

Berry Frappe

1 gallon strawberry ice cream*
1 pint vanilla ice cream
2 cups whole milk
4 cups lemon-lime soda
20 fresh strawberries or 20 sprigs fresh mint

Let ice cream soften on countertop for 15 minutes. Place the softened ice cream in a large container and blend with the milk using a steel spoon or hand mixer.

When the ice cream is well blended, pour in the soda and mix only enough to incorporate it. (Mixing too much will make the soda go flat and destroy the bubbly texture.) Pour the frappe into chilled glasses and serve garnished with a fresh berry or mint sprig. Makes 24 eight-ounce servings.

*Raspberry ice cream can be substituted. Garnish with mint sprig or fresh raspberries instead of strawberries.

Mango Otai

16 medium ripe mangos (10 cups cut fruit)
1 quart heavy cream
4 cups pineapple juice
2½ cups coconut cream
½ cup sugar
2½ cups crushed ice

Peel and chop the mangos into small chunks. In a large container or bowl add the mangos, heavy cream, pineapple juice, coconut cream, sugar, and crushed ice. Mix with a large spoon to blend ingredients and dissolve the sugar. Chill in refrigerator or serve immediately. Drink will have to be stirred before serving if it is held in the refrigerator. Makes 24 eight-ounce servings.

Watermelon-Coconut Otai

1 large seedless watermelon (13 cups chopped fruit)
1 quart heavy cream
2 cups water
1½ cups coconut cream
1½ cups sugar
2 cups crushed ice

Peel and chop the watermelon into small chunks. In a large container or bowl add the watermelon, heavy cream, water, coconut cream, sugar, and crushed ice. Mix with a large spoon to blend ingredients and dissolve the sugar. Chill in refrigerator or serve immediately. Drink will have to be stirred before serving if it is held in the refrigerator. Makes 24 eight-ounce servings.

Apple Otai

½ gallon vanilla ice cream
1 quart whole milk
7 Fuji apples, shredded (5 cups shredded fruit)
2½ cups half-and-half
1 40-ounce can fruit cocktail

1 20-ounce can crushed pineapple
2 cups sugar
1 cup coconut flakes
1 liter lemon-lime soda

Let ice cream soften on countertop for 15 minutes. Blend the softened ice cream and remaining ingredients in a large container with a heavy spoon. Chill otai before serving. Drink will need to be stirred just before serving. Makes 24 eight-ounce servings.

Lime Slush

2 cups sugar
8 cups water
1 12-ounce can frozen limeaid
5 fresh limes, juiced
2 12-ounce cans lemon-lime soda

Combine sugar and water in a large saucepan and heat slightly until sugar is dissolved. Add frozen limeaid and juice of 5 limes. Mix and pour into shallow pan. Freeze. Remove from freezer about an hour before serving and break up into slush. Pour into punch bowl and add lemon-lime soda. Makes 18 four-ounce servings.

Cranberry Punch

4 cups cranberry juice cocktail
4 cups apple juice
4 cups sugar-free lemon-lime soda

In a large nonmetal pitcher, stir together cranberry and apple juices. Cover and chill. Just before serving, add lemon-lime soda and stir gently. Makes 24 half-cup servings.

An otai is a traditional Polynesian beverage and a favorite at island gatherings.
Most Polynesian families have their own unique recipes for otais and have been
passing them down through the generations. Experiment with the recipes for
watermelon, apple, and mango otais in this book and create your own tradition.

Wedding Cake

The wedding cake is the crown jewel of your wedding celebration. From a traditional white cake intricately piped with white icing to a spicy carrot cake covered with rich marzipan and brightly colored rose petals to a stacked chocolate extravaganza, your cake should embrace the style of your wedding day.

Often the wedding reception center or caterer will include your wedding cake as part of your package. Other times brides choose to hire a professional baker to create the precise cake they have envisioned. The only limit is your imagination. Ask friends and reception centers for recommendations on bakeries, as not all bakeries can make all kinds of wedding cakes. Also consider asking at fine restaurants in town for recommendations for bakers. Visit bakeries to see examples of their work to make sure you select the right bakery to create your cake. Sometimes a family member or close friend is adventurous and creative enough to make the wedding cake as his or her gift to the bride and groom.

Whatever you decide, take time to look at the different styles and types of wedding cakes that are available to choose from. Whether or not you still opt for a traditional white tiered cake, you will be pleasantly surprised at the many choices for cakes that are available to you.

STYLES OF CAKES

Wedding cakes can range from the very formal to the very simple. They can be elaborate or plain, elegant or fanciful. The most important thing is to choose the wedding cake that best reflects the mood and style of your wedding.

The essence of autumn for example, could be beautifully expressed by creating a country atmosphere for your reception and choosing a spice or pumpkin cake with buttercream frosting in a basket-weave pattern. For an outdoor summer reception, you might choose a cake with fondant rather than buttercream frosting, since fondant will hold up better in warm weather. For the most formal affair, a traditional white tiered cake is still the favorite choice, whether decorated with gum-paste flowers, apricot-colored roses, or gardenias. Elaborate fondant-decorated cakes can serve well in either a formal or more playful setting. The exquisitely formed decorations can create a cake that is uniquely you.

Remember that it is the style, not just the cost, that determines what type of wedding cake you will have. Elaborate cakes can be very expensive and well worth their price, but you can also pick the perfect wedding cake without spending a fortune.

TYPES OF CAKES

Wedding cakes have traditionally been round and three to five tiers high, whether the layers are stacked directly on top of each other or separated by columns. Tiered cakes continue to be the preferred wedding cake, but they can be adapted in a variety of ways. For example, a three-layer cake can be separated with layers of fresh flowers, with the layers of flowers being equally thick as the layers of cake. Roses and lilies would add height, drama, and elegance to your cake. Or for a contemporary look, each tier of your cake can be displayed on a different height cake stand, arranged artistically next to each other.

Cakes need not be layered at all. A single round cake decorated with flowers or sugared fruit makes a beautiful wedding cake, and wedding cakes made to look like hatboxes come in a variety of shapes and sizes. Remember, cakes no longer need be round. Square cakes are in vogue, and you could even create a pyramid or heart-shaped cake.

Frosted pink roses, orchids, and delicate lilies of the valley in detailed icing cascade down this cake, which is topped with a traditional porcelain bride and groom.

TOP LEFT: *A traditional four-tiered cake is dressed up by separating each tier with deep layers of fresh flowers. The beautiful roses and lilies add elegance as well as height to this lovely wedding cake.* TOP RIGHT: *Looped and scrolled frosting is complemented by the four-post column structure of this wedding cake. Its formalness is softened by the light green- and peach-colored tiny fruits and leaves which top each layer.* BOTTOM LEFT: *This traditional buttercream iced cake is covered with soft scrolls, roses, and lilies of the valley rendered in icing. An elongated top layer gives it a slightly modern feel.* BOTTOM RIGHT: *Elaborately detailed in multicolored fondant, this cake has a rich European feel. The small sculpted leaves, grapes, and tiny citrus fruits are reminiscent of an Italian fresco.*

A checkered-look fondant
frosting in yellow and white
is accented with sprightly
gum-paste daisies, giving
this cake a cheerful, springtime feel. Tiny fondant
pearls and a lacy frosting
butterfly add the finishing
touches.

A current trend in cakes is individual wedding cakes. The wedding cake itself is much smaller, and the guests are offered individual cakes that are just the right size for one serving. These cakes are created to reflect the wedding cake, both in ingredients and design. One element from the wedding cake, such as a gum-paste flower, is re-created to decorate each individual cake. Some brides even create an unusual wedding cake for themselves by taking the individual cakes and clustering them together on tiers to resemble a large wedding cake.

Grooms' cakes are also making a comeback. A small cake is made for the groom and displayed at its own table. These cakes can be more whimsical than the formal wedding cake, and often reflect an interest or hobby of the groom, such as golfing, fishing, or a favorite sports car.

FLAVORS, FILLINGS, AND FROSTINGS

In the past, wedding cakes were usually a white or yellow cake with white frosting. Today cakes can be any flavor you desire—from angel food, chocolate, spice, or carrot cake to pound cake, lemon, cherry, banana nut, or even pumpkin.

Fillings of many kinds are also available. Some brides choose cream fillings while others prefer fruit fillings. Whipped cream, chocolate ganache, lemon cream, pineapple, raspberry, or coconut would all make delicious fillings when combined with the right flavor of cake.

The kind of frosting you choose for your wedding cake will greatly determine its style and look. Buttercream frosting is a traditional favorite. It is soft and can

Cakes no longer need be all white. This Wedgwood-blue frosted cake, decorated with brightly colored fresh flowers, is a combination of delightful colors. The white frosting designs of swirls and butterflies add an element of playfulness.

TOP: *Formal columns and elegant fondant calla lilies and gardenias give this cake a classic look.* BOTTOM: *An elaborate display of threads and loops hang over the edges of this three-layer cake. Simple greenery and tiny white stephanotis flowers add beautiful details to the presentation.*

be used to form delicate frosting designs. Fondant frosting is heavier in texture and can be sculpted into elaborate decorations. Marzipan frosting is made from almond paste and sugar. It is also a heavier frosting. As with fondant, marzipan can be molded into fruits and flowers to decorate your cake. Talk with your caterer or baker about the different kinds of frosting and ask to see examples so you can determine which frosting will give your cake the look you desire.

DECORATIONS

Decorations for wedding cakes are no longer limited to scrolls and loops of icing or flowers made of frosting. Fresh flowers, sugared flowers, candy, nuts, fresh fruit, marzipan fruit, or elaborate fondant decorations can grace your cake. The way you choose to decorate your cake is a great opportunity to express your creativity and style.

Fresh flowers can bring an aura of romance to your cake. Pink, red, and orange roses, vibrant orchids, wistful violets, or burnished autumn chrysanthemums add a natural beauty and elegance. Fresh flowers on your cake are a way to restate the flowers used in your wedding bouquet.

Some fresh flowers, such as pansies, rose petals, and nasturtiums are edible. Other flowers are non-toxic and can be used to decorate the cake, but should be removed before serving it to your guests. Toxic flowers should not be used on cakes. If, however, you have a love for a flower such as wisteria, which is toxic, you don't have to be disappointed. Your baker can easily render the flower in frosting.

Created with playfully off-balanced layers and adorned with pink fondant diamond shapes, this Alice in Wonderland cake is a whimsical delight. Fondant scrolls and swirls and sugar-blown bubbles offer the perfect touches to make it complete.

Another enchanting option is sugared flowers. Silk flowers, although not as common, are also a possibility. Consider tiny branches of fresh blossoms to adorn your cake as well. Fresh apricot, cherry, or quince blossoms can be unique and enchanting. Other fresh greenery, such as eucalyptus or clematis, makes unusual cake decorations.

Frosting flowers of fondant or marzipan are also beautiful. A skilled cake decorator knows how to turn these flowers into works of art, making your cake equally beautiful as one adorned with fresh flowers, but touched with a different style.

Frosting flowers often hold up better than fresh flowers. They are an excellent choice if you want to use flowers that may not be in season. Pink peonies in the middle of winter or lilies of the valley in the heat of summer might be just the thing you are looking for. Today most bakers are able to design artful cakes using any flower you choose, whether it be fresh or the sweet result of a talented baker and a batch of frosting.

In addition to flowers, cakes can be decorated with everything from tiny champagne grapes to delicate sugar-blown bubbles. Many fancy and attractive designs can be made from frosting, including bows and buttons, lace, or tiny fondant pearls. A design in frosting may mimic a detail of the wedding dress or the fabric on a bridesmaid's gown. Fondant can be made into fanciful swirls or designs that create the style you want. Likewise, marzipan can be formed into anything from tiny fruits to seashells.

Fresh fruits are also an excellent choice. A pile of sweet berries such as blueberries, blackberries, and

ABOVE: Purple lace and a fresh-flower-and-ribbon cake topper decorate this simple three-layer cake.

TOP LEFT: *This rich chocolate cake is as beautiful as it is delicious. The three-tiered, basketweave cake is frosted with chocolate buttercream frosting and decorated with vibrant flowers and fresh fruits, including starfruit, lemon slices, plump grapes, and shiny apples.* TOP RIGHT: *This unique three-layered cake is coated in creamy fondant and draped with rich chocolate. Tiny gum paste flowers in lavender and white are scattered along the sides of each layer.* BOTTOM LEFT: *Individual wedding cakes, such as the one pictured here, are very popular. The cakes are served as the dessert for a wedding luncheon or dinner and are decorated with a detail from the wedding cake itself.* BOTTOM RIGHT: *Thin layers of tiramisu separated with a rich filling of mascarpone cheese create this Italian wedding cake. Each layer boasts fresh raspberries, blueberries, and blackberries and is separated by entwining raspberry vines and leaves.*

raspberries is not only beautiful but also delicious. The cake can be decorated with entwining berry vines as well. Chocolate dipped strawberries can form an attractive layer and topper for a chocolate fondant cake. A summer wedding suggests a citrus theme, with whole, unpeeled fruits, such as mandarin oranges and kumquats, adorned with lemon leaves, or a mixture of lemons and limes. Fall weddings inspire cakes with glazed pears or cascading sugared grapes.

Nuts, currants, shaved white chocolate, tiny candies, and nonpareils offer endless possibilities for decorating your cake. Ribbons, vines, mint, and other herbs are also ideas to consider.

Cake toppers are a traditional favorite. Many kinds of toppers can be saved to become a permanent memento of your wedding cake. Couples often choose the ever-favorite porcelain bride and groom. These can be purchased new, or vintage ones found at flea markets and online auctions. A bride might consider a cake topper used by her mother or a close family friend. Other options are fresh or frosting flowers, fresh or sugared fruit, marzipan decorations, or a repeated motif from the wedding cake. You could also use handmade paper, glass or satin wedding bells, silk doves, or a tiny arbor or wreath.

DISPLAY

Displaying your cake is important. Whether it is set on a silver tray, crystal platter, or antique cake stand, it should be situated in a way that shows it off to best advantage. Place your cake in a prominent position, where guests can admire it. You can decorate the table and the base of the cake by adorning it with ivy, grapevines, garlands, rose petals, sugar-blown balls, candles, or other decorations. Individual wedding cakes and grooms' cakes should be displayed in a separate location.

CUTTING THE CAKE

At many receptions, cutting the cake is the climax of the celebration, a time when the room becomes hushed and the attention is focused solely on the bride and groom. The tradition of the bride and groom cutting the cake symbolizes the couple's first "breaking of bread" together and the promise to nourish each other, both physically and emotionally, throughout their lives.

Decide ahead of time what you will use to cut the cake. Caterers often provide fancy cutting and serving implements. Some brides simply use a knife from the kitchen, while others choose to have their cake knife as a memento of the wedding. They buy a beautiful silver knife and cake server and have them engraved with their initials and wedding date.

The cake is often cut at the very end of the wedding reception. The bride and groom should decide beforehand if they want the cake served to all the guests as part of the refreshments or mostly just to the family. This will determine in large part the size of cake you buy. For example, at a formal sit-down wedding dinner, the cake might be served as the dessert to each guest present. At a bigger reception, if you wait until the very end to cut your cake, the majority of guests may already have left for the evening. One option is to box slices of the wedding cake for guests to take home. Baker supply

stores or caterers should be able to provide boxes that are created for just this purpose. Tradition states that a girl who takes home a slice of wedding cake and sleeps with it under her pillow will dream that night of the man she is going to marry.

There are a few simple guidelines to keep in mind when cutting your cake. First remove the top tier. This is usually frozen and saved for the couple's first anniversary. (The top tier is not figured into the amount of servings a cake will provide.) Cut the first slice from the second tier.

When cutting round tiers into slices for the guests, move in two inches from the tier's outer edge and then cut a circle all the way around the cake. Slice the ring you have created in one- to three-inch pieces. Then move in another two inches and cut another circle, and so on.

RECIPES AND TIPS

If baking your own cake for a wedding, the following information will be helpful.

• Bake a smaller wedding cake and then serve guests from sheet cakes, rather than trying to create a cake big enough to serve all your guests.

• In hot weather, icings can be extra soft. Try adding 4 tablespoons of melted white chocolate to your buttercream. This will help stabilize your icing.

• Use unsalted butter in your icings. You will have more control over taste. It allows the desired flavor to mellow.

If your cake will be displayed outdoors, consider using a thicker fondant frosting and make certain that you display the cake under a covered arbor or tent. ABOVE LEFT: This beautiful cake plays off the flowers in the surrounding garden—daisies, roses, and lilies—which gives it a casual, spring-like feel. ABOVE RIGHT: Many brides purchase a beautiful silver or crystal cake knife and serving implement for the wedding, like the ones pictured here.

• Edible flowers are becoming more popular with cakes. It is crucial to know how they have been cared for. Most flowers that are purchased at nurseries or florists have been sprayed with pesticides and should not be eaten. Produce companies and farmer's markets are a better choice for a supplier.

• You will have fewer crumbs when icing if you bake the cake the day before and freeze it.

• Fill and ice layers before assembling cake.

• Do not assemble cake until you are at the reception site. When transporting tiers, place cakes on damp towels or carpet foam and drive carefully.

• When assembling cake, remember that for heavy cakes a sturdy cake base must be used. Each tier must be on a cardboard, foam board, or plastic divider. Smear each divider with a few strokes of icing to secure cake.

• Don't forget to use dowel rods for support.

• Before placing a layer of cake on its base, sprinkle the base with a little super-fine coconut. This will help prevent sticking.

Wedding Cake

3 egg whites
1½ cups water
¼ teaspoon lemon flavoring
¼ teaspoon orange flavoring
½ teaspoon almond flavoring
1 teaspoon vanilla flavoring
1 box white cake mix
¼ cup all-purpose flour
¼ cup shortening

In a large mixing bowl place the egg whites, water, and flavorings. In a separate bowl, mix the cake mix and flour together, then add to the liquid ingredients. Add the shortening and mix on low speed until moist. Turn the mixer to medium speed and beat for two

ABOVE: Thick, cream-colored fondant covers this cake. The fondant bow and draped layer give the look of rich satin cloth, while the sugared baubles provide a fairytale feel.

minutes. Cake batter should be thick; it should not be thin and runny.

The yield for this recipe is six cups batter. See chart to determine how much batter you will need for the size of wedding cake you want to make. You may need to double or triple this recipe, and so on. See the chart below for baking temperatures and times.

Those at high altitudes should follow the high altitude instructions on the back of the white cake mix box.

Sponge Cake Variation: Replace water with milk for a little more dense cake.

White Buttercream Icing

⅔ cup plus 1 tablespoon water
4 tablespoons meringue powder
12 cups powdered sugar
¾ teaspoon salt
1 teaspoon clear vanilla
1 teaspoon almond flavoring
½ teaspoon lemon flavoring
½ teaspoon orange flavoring
1¼ cups shortening

Combine water and meringue powder; whip at high speed till peaks form. Add 4 cups of the powdered sugar and beat on low speed until well incorporated. Add salt and flavorings; beat slightly. Alternately add shortening and remaining powdered sugar. Beat on low speed until smooth. Makes 7½ cups frosting. See chart below to determine how much icing you will need for the size wedding cake you want to make.

Wedding Cake Baking Chart

SIZE	SERVINGS	CUPS BATTER*	BAKING TEMPERATURE	BAKING TIME
6"	14	2	350° F.	25 minutes
8"	25	3	350° F.	25 to 30 minutes
10"	39	6	350° F.	35 to 40 minutes
12"	56	7	350° F.	35 to 40 minutes
14"	77	10	325° F.	50 to 55 minutes
16"	100	15	325° F.	55 to 60 minutes
18"	127	17	325° F.	60 to 65 minutes

* One cake mix yields 4 to 6 cups of batter. Pans are usually filled two-thirds full.

Wedding Cake Icing Chart

SIZE CAKE	CUPS ICING
6"	3
8"	4
10"	5
12"	6
14"	7+
16"	8+
18"	10+

It is not only necessary to love, it is necessary to say so.
—French saying

A small favor for your guests to take home is not required but is a lovely gesture. What you choose to bestow is not as important as that it was made and presented with thoughtful care. Favors are a simple way to thank guests for sharing your special day with you and are sweet reminders of the celebration.

Many brides choose to give favors at a wedding luncheon or formal wedding dinner, where the guest list is a more intimate gathering of family and close friends. This allows you to put more time and money into meaningful keepsakes than if you tried to give a favor to every guest at a larger scale wedding reception. However, some brides opt to send home small favors with everyone who attends their reception.

Remember that with these tokens, what's on the outside is just as important as what's on the inside. Presentation is everything! Use ribbons, wrapping, boxes, bows, and bags to the best advantage. A wedding favor is another way to restate your wedding theme, so think of gifts that fit the style or mood of your wedding and wrap them in colors and ribbons that match the day.

Favors can be distributed in different ways. You can set the small gifts at each place setting at a luncheon or dinner. In this case, they can double as place cards or dress up a table setting. Alternatively, you can carefully bundle or prettily pile gifts together on a table at a convenient location for guests to take one on their way home.

CANDIES AND FRUITS

Always a popular favor, candies can be dressed up or dressed down, boxed or packaged in a multitude of different ways. Candy boxes can often double as place cards at a sit down luncheon or dinner. Consider having a talented calligrapher inscribe the guests' names on the box or on a place card affixed to the box. There are also a number of different computer fonts and pretty card stocks that can be used to create nice place cards to go with your boxed gifts.

A tiny box of chocolates, wrapped in gold or silver foil and tied with a sheer French ribbon, can be displayed next to the place setting. A cluster of such boxes can also make a charming table of its own. Some couples choose to have the bride and groom's initials monogrammed onto chocolates in gold. For a more casual affair, chocolates can double as place card holders. Make small paper flags on thick card stock with the guests' names. Affix each flag to a toothpick and insert it into the chocolate. Display at each place setting on a small paper doily. If they are in season, nothing is as elegant as a chocolate-dipped strawberry or a cluster of chocolate-dipped raspberries to finish the meal.

Fruits of all kinds make rich and mouthwatering favors. Look to the season for ideas on colors and types of fruits you might want to use. For example, a handful of brightly colored cherries placed in an open velum bag or bunched in a small wicker basket says summer and can add a splash of color to any table setting. Frosted or baked pears make a nice favor for autumn, while a half-pint bottle of homemade peaches or berry jam tied with a gingham ribbon would make a fun favor at a country wedding.

Jordan almonds are a traditional wedding candy. The candy-coated nuts come in a variety of colors and can easily be purchased in the color of your wedding. Place small handfuls in clear white netting and tie with ribbon, wrap in cellophane bags, or place bowls filled with the candies at tables around the room. Colored mints can be handled in a similar fashion. Or if you pre-fer, small boxes of sandwich mints can be elaborately wrapped and handed to the guests as they leave.

A trendy idea for candy favors is to have a table with a grouping of glass canisters of different sizes and shapes, each filled with a different candy. All white candies are often preferred, but any color will work as long as the tones look good together and match your wedding theme. The table holds a candy scoop and small velum or cellophane bags. Guests can help themselves to a scoop of candy upon leaving the reception.

FLOWERS AND PLANTS

There is nothing better than flowers to bring the romance of your wedding to your guests. Flowers can be given in a variety of different ways as favors. At a formal black-and-white affair, a single white rose laid across the dinner plate makes a dramatic statement. At a more casual wedding, a bunch of wildflowers tied with ribbon to the back of each guest's chair achieves the desired effect. Other ways to bring flower favors to your guests include a tiny bud vase of lilies of the valley or violets at each place setting, a calla lily or iris tucked in a tied napkin, or a brightly colored peony or rose handed to each woman as she leaves. Be sure to use blooms that match the other flowers and the style of your wedding.

For a Christmas wedding, consider providing your guests with a sprig of fresh mistletoe or a small bunch of holly tied with red ribbon. For a summer wedding, bunches of fresh herbs, such as lavender, chives, or rosemary, make sweet reminders of the special day. A potted amaryllis bulb sent home with a guest in winter

TOP: *Edible favors are always a favorite. A heart-shaped cookie on a heart-shaped plate, flower cookies in a brown bag, small bags of colored popcorn, or sachets filled with individually wrapped candies are just a few of the limitless choices.* BOTTOM: *Chocolates in cleverly wrapped boxes or Jordan almonds in clear cellophane bags make excellent wedding favors.*

will provide a burst of color at their home a few weeks later.

Some brides use potted flowers or plants as part of their table decorations and then urge the guests to take a plant with them as they leave. Be creative. Geraniums in terra-cotta pots, pansies in painted containers, or dark green shrubbery in galvanized tin buckets are just a few ideas of how you can use your imagination to create the décor of your wedding day and a lasting memento for your guests.

PAPER AND GLASS

Many creative and fun remembrances can be made of paper. Handmade paper bags for each guest can hold the menu for the wedding dinner or conceal a handwritten thank-you note. Origami favors are also a favorite. The intricately folded paper has a charm of its own. Origami swans are a nice choice for a wedding, since swans are one of the few animals in nature that mate for life. Some brides make handmade paper cards or coasters with a favorite quotation or saying, or with the couple's initials or wedding date. A handmade bookmark with a poem, scripture, or saying that is meaningful to you is also an option. There are countless love sonnets and poems—find one that captures your feelings for your beloved and have it inscribed on a bookmark or card to share with everyone. Be sure to use colors and a style that matches your wedding theme.

A simple thank you note should not be overlooked as a thoughtful and appropriate wedding favor. This is different than the thank you note you will send for gifts received; a handwritten note given in person on the day of your wedding thanking your loved one for sharing it

LEFT: What flower girl wouldn't appreciate a delicate glass slipper full of candy as a token of thanks for her participation in your big day. RIGHT: A Christmas ornament, origami swan, or handmade bookmark make unusual wedding favors. Handmade paper boxes of all sizes can add a creative touch to your small tokens of appreciation.

with you may be the most treasured wedding favor of all. If the note is on thick paper and the name carefully and elegantly penned on the envelope, this note could double as a place card as well.

There are also interesting possibilities for favors made of glass. A December wedding suggests a glass Christmas ornament. It could be etched with the couple's names and wedding day or simply be a beautiful ornament that would make a pleasant reminder of the festivities. A snow globe makes a playful winter favor that is sure to be appreciated. Or consider a glass or crystal handheld bell at each place setting as a lovely, formal wedding favor.

BAKED GOODS

Baked goods can be some of the most fun favors if you decide to go this route. Decorated sugar cookies are always a favorite. Small cookies in every imaginable shape and size are a perfect way to repeat your wedding theme. Flowers, bells, hearts, and buttons—the shape of the cookie and how you decorate it has limitless possibilities. Consider using icing (instead of frosting) for more detailed work or use a professional bakery to get the look you desire. Decorate cookies with the couple's initials, tiny hearts, or something completely unique. Cookies can be placed in boxes, bags, or tins, or displayed on trays or serving platters.

Individual wedding cakes are very popular. Have your baker make enough tiny cakes for each of your guests. The cakes match the actual wedding cake and are a perfect and tasty reminder to take home.

For fall weddings, miniature loaves of banana, pumpkin, or zucchini bread capture the flavor of the season. Wrap in cellophane and tie with a matching

LEFT: This elegant pewter vase is filled with white hydrangea, a fragrant and generous gift for guests at a formal wedding breakfast or dinner. RIGHT: Fresh berries in tiny galvanized tin buckets, homemade muffins, or fresh fruit can double as colorful favors and appealing place cards.

ribbon. A basket filled with miniature muffins is a fun favor for a wedding breakfast.

For an Italian dinner, make or buy fancy thin breadsticks that can be tucked in a folded napkin or placed across a salad plate. Or a box of crackers, wafers, or shortbread, cleverly wrapped, can make nice wedding favors.

A romantic favor idea is a small custom-made box containing a slice of the actual wedding cake for guests to take home. Guests often don't get to sample the wedding cake because they are too full from the other refreshments or leave right after the cake is cut. After cutting the cake, have the cake sliced and boxed and get enough helpers to coordinate so that each box is tied with a pretty ribbon and made available quickly. This makes a perfect wedding favor.

TINY TOKENS

The possibilities for wedding favors are endless. Wedding favors can be as elaborate or as simple as you choose. For the most formal occasion you might consider an engraved silver bell or silver candlestick, while a bunch of cinnamon sticks tied with raffia would be perfect for a country affair. You can make a simple summer favor by sewing small sachet bags and filling them with fresh herbs.

Other ideas for wedding favors include the ever-romantic candle—a votive candle for each guest, or several long, thin tapered candles tied together with ribbon. A handkerchief that has been embroidered with the date, the couple's initials, or a small floral motif from the wedding is also a memorable keepsake. A picture frame that matches your wedding theme would be perfect for

ABOVE LEFT: A sachet of sweet-smelling petals or lavender makes a thoughtful gift for guests to take home. ABOVE RIGHT: Boxes containing favors can be tied with ribbons or raffia or decorated with flowers as pictured here.

the guests to take home to frame a picture from the wedding day.

Confetti to throw at the departing couple is a favorite tradition, and confetti of many kinds can be packaged as a wedding favor. Birdseed can be placed in small sachet bags and the contents tossed at the couple at the end of the evening. Bags can be made of cloth or lace and are a pretty as well as fun gift.

Other brides provide each guest with a bottle of blowing bubbles. A sky full of floating bubbles can make a fairytale-like escape for the couple as they leave the reception. For a summer night departure, or after-dark

winter sendoff, have guests light sparklers and stand in a row, lighting the path to the couple's car with magical firelight.

And perhaps the most elegant of all confetti—boxed rose petals. Sweet-smelling petals matching the colors of the wedding, boxed to perfection and tied with beautiful ribbon, make a lovely token of remembrance.

In any case where you will throw confetti or have send-off activities, be sure to use caution and common-sense. If you are having your reception at a rented site or church house, check first to be sure such activities are not prohibited.

ABOVE LEFT: Candles, potpourri, or decorative vinegar bottles would each make a thoughtful wedding favor. ABOVE RIGHT: A fall wedding is the perfect occasion for using harvest fruits as place cards or wedding favors. This pear makes a simple yet beautiful favor to be left on each guest's plate.

After all the planning, organizing, shopping, and showers, there are still a few important things to remember to guarantee a truly successful wedding day.

USING PROFESSIONALS

Many brides—and many more mothers of the bride—make the common mistake of trying to do everything themselves. This is a day for you to celebrate and cherish. It is well worth the expense to hire professionals, from florists to bakers to cleaning crews. It is especially important to hire servers if you will be doing the food for your wedding.

Of course, there may be some aspect of the wedding that you wish to handle yourself, whether it is creating handmade favors or making the wedding veil, but do not try to do it all. It is especially important to have help with the food. The mother of the bride and other family members should be free to mingle with the guests and help the bride enjoy her day, and not be stuck behind the scenes in the kitchen. If you overload yourself you will be stressed out and will miss the joy of one of the most memorable days in your life.

MANAGING STRESS

Partly because your wedding day is such an all-important day that you have dreamed of all your life, and partly because it is such a huge organizational challenge, it inevitably brings about a lot of stress. Don't get so caught up in the stress and worry that you forget to enjoy the day. If you've planned and coordinated everything in advance, and enlisted the right help, by the time the event has actually arrived there is probably little more you can do. Try to relax and enjoy yourself. You are surrounded with friends and loved ones celebrating a joyful event in your life. If little things go wrong—which they almost inevitably will—think of them as great stories to laugh about later rather than being distressed by them. Relax and laugh. Enjoy your special day.

Once you have planned your reception and the big day arrives, try to relax and enjoy the beauty of the day. Pay attention to the things your guests will notice—from the bows on the back of each chair to the centerpieces to the small mementos you give away as favors—and congratulate yourself on planning the perfect celebration for you and your new husband.

You should also consider ways to relax in the days before the wedding. Such things as getting a professional massage, making sure you are getting enough sleep, and setting a time to go to lunch with your sweetheart and *not* talk about wedding plans will help you reach your wedding day happy, refreshed, and beautiful.

KEEPING PERSPECTIVE

It is so easy to get caught up in all the coordinating and work of putting together a wedding that at times you can lose sight of what's really important. Remember that it is the *marriage,* not the wedding reception, that is what this is all about.

Be patient with your family during your engagement and wedding planning process. Realize this is an emotional time for everyone and those people closest to you are just trying to help. They also may be worried about how all the new relationships are going to work once you are married. Your marriage affects a lot of people besides you and your future husband. And remember, everyone feels exasperated with their in-laws at one time or another!

Don't let the celebration overshadow the eternal significance of the day. When you keep your focus on your fiancé and the commitment you are making to each other, little complications won't really seem that important.

FREQUENTLY ASKED QUESTIONS

When should I mail out the wedding invitations?

Wedding invitations are traditionally mailed out four to six weeks before the wedding. It has become acceptable in Latter-day Saint culture, however, to mail out invitations three to four weeks in advance. Whatever you do, be careful not to mail out invitations any later than three weeks in advance.

Who should I invite to the temple?

The temple sealing is a very personal and private ceremony and only family members and close friends should be invited. The sealing rooms vary in size, and you will want to contact the temple in advance to arrange for a room that accommodates the number of guests you plan to include.

What about family members who aren't able to attend the temple?

Be sure that family members, as well as close friends, who will not be attending the temple feel important and included on your wedding day. Invite them to join you on the temple grounds at the approximate time you will be coming out of the temple so they can give their congratulations and be included in the photographs. Let them know if they don't want to come to the temple grounds that they are invited to the wedding breakfast, ring ceremony, or any other special events to celebrate the day.

Who should I invite to the wedding breakfast?

You will want to include family members and close friends in your wedding breakfast. Anyone who has been invited to the temple sealing should have an invitation. In addition, the wedding breakfast is an opportunity to include close family members and friends that are not attending the temple. Make sure you accommodate both the bride and the groom's family and friends when planning your guest list.

Do I have to have a traditional wedding reception?

No. Many couples choose a formal wedding dinner in lieu of a reception. Other couples take the money that would have been spent on a reception and use it for a honeymoon or a down payment on a home. Whatever you choose, make sure it is a mutual choice both the bride and the groom feel good about.

Should my bridesmaids stand in line or mill about?

The current trend is for bridesmaids to mill around the reception during the evening instead of standing in a formal line. However, the more traditional receiving line is fine if you prefer. In either case, the bride and groom (and usually their parents) should stand in line so guests can offer their congratulations in a more formal and organized setting.

What is the etiquette for cutting the cake?

The tradition of feeding each other a piece of the first slice of wedding cake is an age-old one. Some couples tend to get carried away and smear cake in each other's faces. Remember that the way you feed each other at this moment can be seen as a symbol of how you will treat each other in your marriage. Be

mature—this can be a very romantic moment if you let it be one.

If you do wish to have a bit of fun with the frosting, however, you should talk to each other in advance so you both know what to expect and one person isn't ruining the moment for the other. And be sure to respect each other's wishes.

Should I insist on what the mothers wear?

It is appropriate to give the mothers of the bride and groom a color, or a color scheme, you would like them to follow. After that, they need to be able to pick their own dresses in a style that they like and are comfortable wearing.

How should I get my in-laws to meet my parents?

It is nice if the parents of the engaged couple can meet right away, although that is not always possible. You may want to arrange a dinner at your home, your parents' home, or at a restaurant. If parents live far away from each other, you might want to arrange for a phone conversation. And in cases of divorce and remarriage, you might have several different get-togethers before everyone meets. If you do go out to dinner, be clear beforehand on who is paying for what.

What should I give for bridesmaid gifts?

Give a keepsake that is permanent. Many brides give earrings or a necklace that can be worn the night of the reception. A picture frame, jewelry box, vase, or candlesticks are just a few other possibilities.

Should my husband and I exchange wedding gifts?

It sometimes can be difficult to come up with wedding gifts for each other, since you have already spent so much money and since the perfect gift is hard to decide on. However, try to think of wedding gifts to exchange. It starts your wedding on the note of giving to each other; the gifts will be important heirlooms for your children and grandchildren; and they are symbolic of the most important gift you will give on your wedding day—the gift of yourselves.

Who plans the honeymoon?

The bride and groom usually plan the honeymoon together, with the groom taking the lead. Sometimes the groom likes to plan the honeymoon as a surprise. Be sure you agree beforehand on how you want to handle the planning for your honeymoon. And be honest with each other about what you want; that is much better than later regretting you didn't speak up.

Who pays for what?

Although you can divide up the costs of a wedding in different ways as long as it is acceptable to both parties, traditionally wedding costs are assigned as follows. (Note: When it indicates "bride" it means the bride or the family of the bride; when it indicates "groom" it means the groom or the family of the groom.)

ITEM	WHO PAYS
Engagement ring	Groom
Bride's wedding ring	Groom
Groom's wedding ring	Bride
Invitations or announcements	Bride
Bride's dress and accessories	Bride
Bridesmaids' dresses	Bride (or the bridesmaids may pay for their own)
Groom's tuxedo and accessories	Groom
Tuxedos for groomsmen and fathers	Groom (or the groomsmen may pay for their own)
Dresses for the mothers	The mothers usually pay for their own
Costs for the reception: including reception center, food, centerpieces, and so on	Bride
Costs for open house	Groom (but if the bride's family is giving the open house then the costs are assumed by the bride)
Wedding cake	Bride
Photography	Bride
Bridesmaids' flowers and mothers' corsages	Bride
Bridal bouquet and boutonnières	Groom
Gift for the bride	Groom
Gift for the groom	Bride
Gifts for the bridesmaids	Bride
Gifts for the groomsmen	Groom
Honeymoon	Groom

CREDITS

Photos by Alan Blakely and John Luke. Additional photos by Comstock, Photodisc, Design Werks, and Shauna Gibby.

The following businesses and individuals deserve credit and thanks for providing the materials and settings photographed on these pages. Contact information can be found on page 139. Images that are not referred to come courtesy of Comstock and Photodisc.

Receptions:

PAGE viii: Joseph Smith Memorial Building. **PAGE 2:** *top:* Joseph Smith Memorial Building; *bottom:* Design Werks. **PAGE 3:** Lion House. **PAGE 4:** *left and right:* Joseph Smith Memorial Building. **PAGE 5:** *top middle and bottom:* Joseph Smith Memorial Building; *top right:* Carrie Biggers, Carrie's Cakes. **PAGE 7:** *top and bottom:* Design Werks. **PAGE 8:** *top left and right:* Joseph Smith Memorial Building; *bottom left and right:* Design Werks. **PAGE 9:** *left:* Design Werks; *right:* Joseph Smith Memorial Building. **PAGE 10:** *left:* Joseph Smith Memorial Building; *right:* Design Werks. **PAGE 11:** *top left and bottom right:* Design Werks; *top right and bottom left:* Joseph Smith Memorial Building. **PAGE 12:** Design Werks. **PAGE 13:** *top and bottom:* Design Werks. **PAGE 14:** *left and middle:* Joseph Smith Memorial Building; *right:* Design Werks. **PAGE 15:** Design Werks. **PAGE 16:** Lion House. **PAGE 19:** *top right and bottom left:* Joseph Smith

Memorial Building. **PAGE 20:** *right:* Joseph Smith Memorial Building. **PAGE 21:** *left and right:* Joseph Smith Memorial Building. **PAGE 22:** *all images:* Joseph Smith Memorial Building. **PAGE 23:** *right:* Joseph Smith Memorial Building. **PAGE 24:** *middle:* Joseph Smith Memorial Building; *right:* Design Werks. **PAGE 25:** *top left:* Design Werks; *bottom right:* Joseph Smith Memorial Building. **PAGE 26:** *bottom:* Design Werks. **PAGE 27:** *bottom:* Barbara Wachs, Exclusive Cakes by Barbara. **PAGE 32:** *bottom:* Lion House. **PAGE 33:** *bottom:* Temple Square gardens.

Flowers:

PAGE 34: Roots. **PAGE 37:** *all images:* Joseph Smith Memorial Building Floral Department. **PAGE 38:** Roots. **PAGE 39:** *right:* Skyline Flower Gardens. **PAGE 41:** *top middle:* Joseph Smith Memorial Building; *bottom:* Huddart Floral. **PAGE 42:** Joseph Smith Memorial Building Floral Department. **PAGE 43:** Joseph Smith Memorial Building Floral Department. **PAGE 44:** Brown Floral. **PAGE 45:** *bottom left:* Joseph Smith Memorial Building Floral Department. **PAGE 47:** *top left:* Huddart Floral; *top right:* Roots; *bottom, clockwise from top left:* Joseph Smith Memorial Building Floral Department; Brown Floral; Roots; Joseph Smith Memorial Building Floral Department. **PAGE 48:** *top and bottom:* Joseph Smith Memorial Building Floral Department. **PAGE 49:** Joseph Smith Memorial Building

Floral Department. **PAGE 50:** *left and right:* Joseph Smith Memorial Building Floral Department.

Food:

A&Z Produce in Salt Lake City provided the fresh produce used in these pictures. The following individuals loaned us dishes for the food photos: Rebecca Crookston, Maxine Bramwell, Annette Dickman, Shauna Gibby, Jody Hazen, Linnae Peterson, and Steve Kachocki.

PAGE 56: Joseph Smith Memorial Building. **PAGE 58:** *left:* Design Werks; *right:* Joseph Smith Memorial Building. **PAGE 59:** *left and right:* Joseph Smith Memorial Building. **PAGE 60:** *top:* Joseph Smith Memorial Building; *bottom:* Lion House. **PAGE 63:** *top and bottom:* Joseph Smith Memorial Building. **PAGE 66:** Joseph Smith Memorial Building. **PAGE 68:** Joseph Smith Memorial Building. **PAGE 71:** Joseph Smith Memorial Building. **PAGE 72:** Lion House. **PAGE 74:** *top:* Lion House; *bottom:* Joseph Smith Memorial Building. **PAGE 77:** *top and bottom:* Lion House. **PAGE 79:** *top and bottom:* Joseph Smith Memorial Building. **PAGE 81:** Joseph Smith Memorial Building. **PAGE 82:** Lion House. **PAGE 86:** *top and bottom:* Joseph Smith Memorial Building. **PAGE 88:** *left and right:* Joseph Smith Memorial Building. **PAGE 91:** *top left and right:* Lion House; *bottom:* Joseph Smith Memorial Building. **PAGE 94:** Joseph Smith Memorial Building. **PAGE 97:** *left and right:* Joseph Smith Memorial Building. **PAGE 98:** *top and bottom left:* Lion House; *bottom right:* Joseph Smith Memorial Building. **PAGE 101:** Lion House. **PAGE 104:** Joseph Smith Memorial Building. **PAGE 105:** *top:* Lion House; *bottom:* Joseph Smith Memorial Building. **PAGE 106:** *top:* Lion House; *bottom:* Joseph Smith Memorial Building. **PAGE 109:** Joseph Smith Memorial Building.

Cakes:

PAGE 110: Cake: Barbara Wachs, Exclusive Cakes by Barbara, flowers: Joseph Smith Memorial Building Floral Department.

PAGE 112: Mrs. Backer's Pastry Shop.
PAGE 113: *top left:* Carrie Biggers, Carrie's Cakes; *top right:* Linda Gerlach; *bottom left:* Karin Kellgreen, Joseph Smith Memorial Building; *bottom right:* Maha, Pastry Arts Barrani.
PAGE 114: Barbara Wachs, Exclusive Cakes by Barbara. **PAGE 115:** Maha, Pastry Arts Barrani. **PAGE 116:** *top:* Barbara Wachs, Exclusive Cakes by Barbara; *bottom:* Lisa Flinders, Mrs. Flinders Cakes. **PAGE 117:** Jaynie Maxfield, Ambrosia. **PAGE 118:** Barbara Wachs, Exclusive Cakes by Barbara. **PAGE 119:** *top left:* Julie Ulrich, Lion House; *top right:* Karin Kellgreen, Joseph Smith Memorial Building; *bottom left:* Jody Cory, Joseph Smith Memorial Building; *bottom right:* Bakers de Normandie.
PAGE 121: *left:* cake: Barbara Wachs, Exclusive Cakes by Barbara, flowers: Design Werks; *right:* Joseph Smith Memorial Building. **PAGE 122:** Barbara Wachs, Exclusive Cakes by Barbara.

Favors:

PAGE 124: Hazen Design. **PAGE 127:** Hazen Design. **PAGE 128:** Hazen Design. **PAGE 129:** *left:* Joseph Smith Memorial Building; *right:* Hazen Design. **PAGE 130:** *right:* Lion House. **PAGE 131:** Hazen Design.

Tips:

PAGE 132: Joseph Smith Memorial Building Floral Department. **PAGE 134:** *top:* Joseph Smith Memorial Building.

Credits:

PAGE 139: *left-hand column: cake:* Barbara Wachs, Exclusive Cakes by Barbara; *flowers:* Design Werks.

Resources:

PAGE 139: *middle column:* Joseph Smith Memorial Building Floral Department. **PAGE 140:** *right-hand column:* Hazen Design.

Index:

PAGE 144: *left-hand column:* Carriage for Hire.

RESOURCES

Lion House
63 East South Temple Street
Salt Lake City, UT 84150
(801) 363-5466
www.lion-house.com
Receptions, wedding breakfasts, luncheons, dinners, buffets, flowers, cakes, decorations

Joseph Smith Memorial Building
15 East South Temple Street
Salt Lake City, UT 84111
(800) 881-5762 (toll free)
(801) 539-3130
www.jsmb.com
Receptions, wedding breakfasts, luncheons, dinners, buffets, flowers, cakes, decorations

Design Werks
76 South Orchard Drive
North Salt Lake, UT 84054
(801) 936-3674
www.deswerks.com
Wedding consultation and planning, decorations, props, flowers

Brown Floral
2233 East Murray-Holladay Road
Salt Lake City, UT 84117
(801) 278-4800
Flowers, bouquets, centerpieces

Huddart Floral Co.
156 East 900 South
Salt Lake City, UT 84111
(801) 531-7900
www.huddartfloral.com
Flowers, bouquets, centerpieces

Roots
360 South Rio Grande
Salt Lake City, UT 84101
(801) 363-7668
Flowers, bouquets, centerpieces

Skyline Flower Gardens
3398 Highland Drive
Salt Lake City, UT 84106
(801) 466-8118
Flowers, bouquets, centerpieces

Carriage for Hire
428 West 200 North
Salt Lake City, UT 84103
801-363-8687
www.carriageforhire.net
Horse-drawn carriage rides

Ambrosia Cakes by Jaynie Maxfield
118 South 2625 East
Layton, UT 84040
(801) 546-2959
Cakes

Bakers de Normandie
4679 South Holladay Boulevard
Holladay, UT 84117
(801) 277-5244
and
2075 South 700 East
Salt Lake City, UT 84105
(801) 484-1251
Cakes

Carrie's Cakes
1454 East Ridgemark Drive
Sandy, UT 84092
(801) 517-1620
www.carriesweddingcakes.com
Cakes, catering, invitations

Exclusive Wedding Cakes by Barbara
755 East Winchester
Murray, UT 84107
(801) 262-0977
www.exclusiveweddingcakes.com
Cakes

Julie Ulrich
(801) 539-3252
Cakes

Linda Gerlach
(801) 942-1043
Cakes

Mrs. Backer's Pastry Shop
434 East South Temple Street
Salt Lake City, UT 84111
(801) 532-2022
Cakes

Mrs. Flinders Cakes
1398 North 75 West
Centerville, UT 84014
(801) 292-9639
Cakes

Pastry Arts Barrani
By appointment
332 East 900 South
Salt Lake City, UT 84111
(801) 596-3353
Cakes

Hazen Design
2526 East Antelope Drive
Layton, UT 84040
(801) 593-8182
Favors, interior design, floral design

RECIPE INDEX

Boldface numbers indicate a page with a photograph.

Quiche, ham, 62, **68**

Raspberry cheesecake, **98**
Refrigerator rolls, 92
Relish, apricot cranberry, 103
Ribbon sandwich, 103, **105**
Rice pilaf, **74**
Risotto, confetti, **71**, 73
Roast turkey breast tea sandwiches, 103, **105**
Roasted potatoes, 83
Rolls: Lion House, 76; refrigerator, 92

Salad: apple pomegranate, 84; fresh mozzarella and tomato, 90, **91**; fruit, 66; grapefruit and avocado, **74**, 75; mixed green, **79**; potato, 92–93; snowpea cucumber, **71**, 75–76; Waldorf, 92
Salmon, with pineapple raspberry salsa, **56**, 78, **79**
Salsa: fruit, 64; pineapple raspberry, **56**, 78, **79**
Sandwiches: bacon and tomato, **74**; open face, 90; ribbon, 103, **105**; roast turkey breast, 103, **105**
Satay sauce, 89
Sauces: apricot cranberry, 70; balsamic apple, 70; hollandaise, 65;

Hunter, 78–79; mushroom, for chicken, 80; orange marmalade, 88; Orientale, 87; pineapple, for ham, **60**, 70; Satay, 89
Shrimp: coconut, 87–88; crostini, **86**, 87; wonton wrapped, **86–87**

Slush, lime, 108
Snowpea cucumber salad, **71**, 75–76
Spreads: almond-bacon cheese, 90; chicken salad, 104; cream cheese, 104; green chili artichoke, 90; ham, 90
Squash, sautéed summer, 83
Stabilized whipping cream, 85
Sting of the bee cake, **98**, 99–100, **101**
Strawberries: dipped, 97, **98**, **106**; tuxedo dipped, **94**, **97**
Strawberry frappe, **106**
Strawberry tarts, **105**, 106–7
Stuffing, for chicken, 80
Swedish meatballs, 89

Tarts: fruit, **94**, 96; strawberry, **105**, 106–7
Toffee torte, **98**, 100
Torte: lemon coconut, **77**, **98**, 100; toffee, **98**, 100
Turkey, roast, tea sandwiches, 103

Vanilla pudding, 95
Vegetable medley, 74
Vegetables: fresh string green beans, **60**, 74–75; fresh, with dip, **91**; roasted julienne root, **71**, 75; sautéed summer squash medley, 83

Waldorf salad, 92
Watermelon-coconut otai, 108, **109**
Wedding cake, 122–23
Whipping cream, stabilized, 85
White buttercream icing, 123
White cake, **98**
Wonton wrapped shrimp, **86–87**

SUBJECT INDEX

Boldface numbers indicate a page with a photograph.